Focus in Grade 8

Teaching with Curriculum Focal Points

Additional titles in the
Teaching with Curriculum Focal Points series:

The Teaching with Curriculum Focal Points series consists of grade-level publications designed to support teachers, supervisors, and coordinators as they begin the discussion of a more focused curriculum across and within prekindergarten through grade 8, as presented in *Curriculum Focal Points for Prekindergarten through Grade 8 Mathematics.*

	ISBN #	NCTM stock #
Focus in Prekindergarten	978-0-87353-644-8	13626
Focus in Kindergarten	978-0-87353-645-5	13627
Focus in Grade 1	978-0-87353-646-2	13628
Focus in Grade 2	Coming Fall 2010	
Focus in Pre-K–2	978-0-87353-624-0	13486
Focus in Grade 3	978-0-87353-625-7	13487
Focus in Grade 4	978-0-87353-627-1	13490
Focus in Grade 5	978-0-87353-614-1	13437
Focus in Grades 3–5	978-0-87353-609-7	13395
Focus in Grade 6	978-0-87353-648-6	13630
Focus in Grade 7	978-0-87353-649-3	13631
Focus in Grades 6–8	978-0-87353-618-9	13465

Please visit www.nctm.org/catalog for details and ordering information.

Focus in Grade 8

Teaching with Curriculum Focal Points

Jane F. Schielack, *Series Advisor*
Texas A&M University

NATIONAL COUNCIL OF
TEACHERS OF MATHEMATICS

Copyright © 2010 by
THE NATIONAL COUNCIL OF TEACHERS OF MATHEMATICS, INC.
1906 Association Drive, Reston, VA 20191-1502
(703) 620-9840; (800) 235-7566; www.nctm.org
All rights reserved

Library of Congress Cataloging-in-Publication Data

Focus in grade 8 : teaching with curriculum focal points.
    p. cm.
ISBN 978-0-87353-650-9
    Includes bibliographical references and index.
    1. Mathematics—Study and teaching (Elementary)—Standards—United States. 2. Education, Elementary—Curricula—Standards—United States. 3. Eighth grade (Education)—Curricula—Standards—United States. 4. Curriculum planning—Standards—United States. I. National Council of Teachers of Mathematics. II. Title: Focus in grade eight.
    QA135.6.F6296 2010
    372.7--dc22

                                    2010005424

The National Council of Teachers of Mathematics is a public voice of mathematics education, supporting teachers to ensure equitable mathematics learning of the highest quality for all students through vision, leadership, professional development, and research.

Printed in the United States of America

Contents

Contents — Continued

On September 12, 2006, the National Council of Teachers of Mathematics released *Curriculum Focal Points for Prekindergarten through Grade 8 Mathematics: A Quest for Coherence* to encourage discussions at the national, state, and district levels on the importance of designing a coherent elementary mathematics curriculum focusing on the important mathematical ideas at each grade level. The natural question that followed the release of *Curriculum Focal Points* was "How do we translate this view of a focused curriculum into the classroom?"

Focus in Grade 8, one in a series of grade-level publications, is designed to support teachers, supervisors, and coordinators as they begin the discussion of a more focused curriculum across and within prekindergarten through grade 8, as presented in *Curriculum Focal Points*. *Focus in Grade 8*, in conjunction with the *Focus in Grade 6* (NCTM 2010) and *Focus in Grade 7* (NCTM 2010) books, will provide a strong foundation for mathematics in a focused curriculum across grades 6 through 8. Important mathematics to prepare students for grade 8 is addressed in the publications *Focus in Grade 6* and *Focus in Grade 7*. Additionally, teacher educators should find *Focus in Grade 8* useful as a vehicle for exploring with their preservice teachers the mathematical ideas and curriculum issues related to the suggested grade 8 Curriculum Focal Points.

The contributors to, and reviewers of, these publications, all active leaders in mathematics education and professional development, guided the creation of this grade-level book as a framework for lesson-study experiences in which teachers deepen their understanding of the mathematical ideas they will be teaching. This book describes and illustrates instructional progressions for the mathematical concepts and skills of each grade 8 Curriculum Focal Point, including powerful representational supports for teaching and learning that can facilitate understanding, stimulate productive discussions about mathematical thinking, and provide a foundation for fluency with the core ideas. Because these instructional progressions cut across grades, you will see the progressions in each grade accompanied by summaries of progressions before and after that grade that connect to Focal Points and Connections in previous and following grades.

Whether you are working with your colleagues or individually, we hope you will find the discussions of the instructional progressions, representations, problems, and lines of reasoning valuable as you plan activities and discussions for your students and as you strive to help your students achieve the depth of understanding of important mathematical concepts necessary for their future success.

—*Jane F. Schielack*
Series Advisor

To address the need for a prototypical, coherent, grade-level-specific mathematics curriculum linked to *Principles and Standards for School Mathematics* (NCTM 2000), the National Council of Teachers of Mathematics asked a team of mathematicians, mathematics educators, and school-based educators to identify three or four focal points in mathematics for each grade level, prekindergarten through grade 8. The writing team—consisting of at least one university-level mathematics educator or mathematician and one pre-K–8 classroom practitioner from each of the three grade bands (pre-K–grade 2, grades 3–5, and grades 6–8)—worked together to create a set of focal points that could serve as areas of emphasis for each grade level and be used as an outline for an articulated pre-K–8 mathematics curriculum. The members of the writing team based their decisions on recommendations from *Principles and Standards*, examinations of multiple curricula from several states and countries, and reviews of a wide array of researchers' and experts' writings on the subject.

We appreciate the contributions of all who have made this document possible.

On behalf of the Board of Directors,

Cathy Seeley
President (2004–2006)
National Council of Teachers of Mathematics

Francis (Skip) Fennell
President, 2006–2008
National Council of Teachers of Mathematics

Members of the Curriculum Focal Points for Grades PK–8 Writing Team

Jane F. Schielack, *Chair*, Texas A&M University, College Station, Texas
Sybilla Beckmann, University of Georgia, Athens, Georgia
Randall I. Charles, San José State University (emeritus), San José, California
Douglas H. Clements, University at Buffalo, State University of New York, Buffalo, New York
Paula B. Duckett, District of Columbia Public Schools (retired), Washington, D.C.
Francis (Skip) Fennell, McDaniel College, Westminster, Maryland
Sharon L. Lewandowski, Bryant Woods Elementary School, Columbia, Maryland
Cathy Seeley, Charles A. Dana Center, University of Texas at Austin, Austin, Texas
Emma Treviño, Charles A. Dana Center, University of Texas at Austin, Austin, Texas
Rose Mary Zbiek, The Pennsylvania State University, University Park, Pennsylvania

Staff Liaison
Melanie S. Ott, National Council of Teachers of Mathematics, Reston, Virginia

ACKNOWLEDGMENTS

The National Council of Teachers of Mathematics would like to thank the following individuals for developing a detailed outline of the content of this publication and for their reviews of, and feedback on, drafts of the manuscript. Special thanks go to Janie Schielack for all her time and support, her invaluable guidance and advice, and her continuing commitment to the Curriculum Focal Points project.

Series Advisor
Jane F. Schielack

Content Development
Words & Numbers
Baltimore, Maryland

Developers
Gladis Kersaint
University of South Florida

Connie Laughlin
Milwaukee, Wisconsin

Jim Lewis
University of Nebraska—Lincoln

Reviewers
Rose Mary Zbiek
Pennsylvania State University

Marshalyn Baker
Messalonskee Middle School
Oakland, Maine

Introduction

Purpose of This Guide

Your first question when looking at NCTM's Curriculum Focal Points might be "How can I use NCTM's Focal Points with the local and state curriculum I am expected to teach?" NCTM's Curriculum Focal Points are not intended to be a national curriculum but have been developed to help bring more consistency to mathematics curricula across the country. Collectively, they constitute a framework of how curricula might be organized at each grade level, prekindergarten through grade 8. They are also intended to help bring about discussion within and across states and school districts about the important mathematical ideas to be taught at each grade level. Because of the current variation among states' curricula, the Curriculum Focal Points are not likely to match up perfectly with any one state's curriculum. This volume explores the mathematics emphasized at grade 8 in the focused curriculum suggested by the NCTM Curriculum Focal Points framework. Additional grade-level and grade-band books are available from NCTM to help teachers translate the Curriculum Focal Points identified for their grade level into coherent and meaningful instruction. Taken together, this grade 8 guide, along with the grades 6 and 7 guides (NCTM 2010) and the grade 6–8 grade-band guide (Mirra 2009), can be used by groups of teachers in professional development experiences as well as by individual classroom teachers.

Purpose of Curriculum Focal Points

The mathematics curriculum in the United States has often been characterized as a "mile wide and an inch deep." Many topics are studied each year—often reviewing much that was covered in previous years—and little depth is added each time the topic is addressed. In addition, because education has always been locally controlled in the United States, learning expectations can significantly differ by state and local school systems. NCTM's *Curriculum Focal Points for Prekindergarten through Grade 8 Mathematics: A Quest for Coherence* (2006) is the next step in helping states and local districts refocus their curriculum. It provides an example of a focused and coherent curriculum in prekindergarten through grade 8 by identifying the most important mathematical topics, or "Focal Points," at each grade level. The Focal Points are not discrete topics to be taught and checked off, but rather a cluster of related knowledge, skills, and concepts. By organizing and prioritizing curriculum and instruction in prekindergarten–grade 8 around Focal Points at each grade level, teachers can foster more cumulative learning of mathematics by students, and students' work in the later grades will build on and deepen what they learned in the earlier grades. Organizing mathematics content in this

A curriculum is more than a collection of activities: It must be coherent, focused on important mathematics, and well articulated across the grades.

—The Curriculum Principle, *Principles and Standards for School Mathematics*

> It provides an example of a focused and coherent curriculum in prekindergarten through grade 8 by identifying the most important mathematical topics, or "Focal Points," at each grade level.

way will help ensure a solid mathematical foundation for high school mathematics and beyond.

Prior to the Curriculum Focal Points, the National Council of Teachers of Mathematics began the process of bringing about change to school mathematics programs in the 1980s, particularly with the first publication to outline standards in mathematics, titled *Curriculum and Evaluation Standards for School Mathematics* (NCTM 1989). That publication provided major direction to states and school districts in developing their curricula. NCTM's *Principles and Standards for School Mathematics* (2000) further elaborated on the ideas of the 1989 Standards, outlining learning expectations in the grade bands of prekindergarten–2, 3–5, 6–8, and 9–12. *Principles and Standards* also highlighted six principles, which included the Curriculum Principle, to offer guidance for developing mathematics programs. The Curriculum Principle emphasized the need to link with, and build on, mathematical ideas as students progress through the grades, deepening their mathematical knowledge over time.

The Impact of Focal Points on Curriculum, Instruction, and Assessment

Significant improvement can be made in the areas of curriculum, instruction, and assessment by identifying Focal Points at each grade level. At the curriculum level, Focal Points will allow for more rigorous and in-depth study of important mathematics at each grade level. This rigor will translate to a more meaningful curriculum that students can understand and apply. At the instructional level, Focal Points will allow teachers to more fully know the core topics they are responsible for teaching. Teachers will not necessarily be teaching *less* or *more* but will be able to teach *better*. Professional development can also be tailored to deepen teachers' knowledge of these Focal Points and connect these ideas in meaningful ways. Assessments can be designed that truly measure students' mastery of core topics rather than survey a broad range of disparate topics, thus allowing for closer monitoring of students' development. At the level of classroom assessment, having a smaller number of essential topics will help teachers have time to better determine what their students have learned and whether they have learned the material deeply enough to use and build on it in subsequent years. If state assessments are more focused as well, more detailed information can be gathered for districts and schools on areas for improvement.

Using This *Focus in Grade 8* Book

Many teachers tell us that they did not have an opportunity in their teacher preparation programs to build sufficient understanding of some of the mathematics topics that they now teach. The discussion of the mathematical ideas presented here is detailed enough for teachers to begin building understanding of the mathematics contained in each grade 8 Focal Point. To further understand what mathematics students are expected to learn before grade 8 and in later grades, teachers would benefit from examining the publications *Focus in Grade 6* (NCTM 2010), *Focus in Grade 7* (NCTM 2010), and *Focus in High School Mathematics: Reasoning and Sense Making* (NCTM 2009). We suggest that teachers form study groups (such as those in lesson study, mathematics circles, or other learning communities) to read and discuss parts of this publication, to work together to build a deeper understanding of the mathematics topics in each Focal Point, and to plan how to help their students develop such understanding by adapting as needed their present grade 8 teaching and learning strategies and materials. A helpful approach for other teacher working groups has been to share students' insights and questions and to look at students' work to understand different ways that students are solving problems, to address errors and misconceptions, and to help students move forward in a progression that fosters both understanding and fluency. Because teachers' lives are busy and demanding, the reader is better served by concentrating on small portions of this publication at a time and working through them deeply instead of trying to do too much at once and getting discouraged. Teachers' learning, like students' learning, is a continual process that can be very rewarding.

Bringing Focus into the Classroom: Instruction That Builds Understanding and Fluency

Although the main goal of this publication is to present in more detail the mathematical content in each of the Focal Points, some important pedagogical issues also need to be taken into account when creating an environment that supports focused instruction. Pedagogical principles for classrooms that do help students build understanding are outlined in *Principles and Standards for School Mathematics* (NCTM 2000) and in the National Research Council reports *Adding It Up* (Kilpatrick, Swafford, and Findell 2001) and *How Students Learn: Mathematics in the Classroom* (Donovan and Bransford 2005). An instructional environment that supports the development of understanding and fluency should be based on a logical progression of content that is connected across grades as well as within grades, should provide opportunities for students and teachers to engage in mathematically substantive discussions, and should involve teachers and students in interpreting and creating mathematical representations to enhance their understanding.

An instructional-progression approach

An instructional progression of concepts and skills supports coherence across and within grades. The table at the beginning of each Focal Point outlines the instructional progression and presents the mathematics suggested for grade 8 within the context of the related mathematics suggested for the grades before and after. Teacher study groups can work to identify gaps in the knowledge of their students that might be causing them difficulties with the mathematics in grade 8. In addition, the instructional progression offers a view of the future mathematics in which students will be applying the knowledge and skills learned in grade 8.

In-depth instructional conversations

Students have little opportunity to build understanding in a classroom in which the teacher does all the talking and explaining. A valuable instructional approach is one in which teachers create a nurturing, meaning-making community as students use "math talk" to discuss their mathematical thinking and help one another clarify their own mathematical thinking, understand and overcome errors, and describe the methods they use to solve problems (Fuson and Murata 2007). Such discussions identify commonalities and differences as well as advantages and disadvantages across methods. By having students talk about their own strategies, teachers can help them become aware of, and build on, their implicit informal knowledge (Lampert 1989; Mack 1990). As the teacher and students learn to listen respectfully to the math talk of others, they model, structure and clarify, instruct or explain, question, and give feedback to enhance one another's learning. As students' understanding and fluency in various topics increase, the amount and type of class discussion related to each topic will change. In-depth discussion of new topics should begin as more sophisticated, mature discussion of previously encountered topics continues.

Using mathematical representations

The use of mathematical representations, in particular mathematical drawings, during problem-solving discussions and explanations of mathematical thinking helps listeners better understand the speaker. The use of mathematical drawings as a component of homework and classwork by both students and the teacher helps them better understand one another's thinking and thus provides continual assessment to guide instruction as the teacher addresses issues that arise in such drawings and accompanying talk (e.g., errors or interesting mathematical thinking). Middle school teachers can use students' prior knowledge as a basis for building new understandings (Webb, Boswinkel, and Dekker 2008). Students can deepen their mathematical understandings by being led to make connections between their own representations that are "often grounded in … experiences with real or imagined contexts" (p. 112) and new, less contextually bound representations purposefully introduced by the teacher. Examples are included throughout this publication as to how grade 8 teachers can help their students make the transition from concrete and numerical representations to algebraic reasoning, generalization, and abstract representations.

An Important Grade 8 Issue: Algebra Readiness

The NCTM Curriculum Focal Points were "designed with the intention of providing a three-year middle school program that includes a full year of general mathematics in each of grades 6, 7, and 8" (p. 10). The many schools that offer a first algebra course in grade 7 or 8 should include the content in the grade 8 Focal Points in earlier grades to enhance students' readiness for algebra. Students who wait until grade 9 to begin their high school mathematics coursework can benefit from productive time spent in grade 8 further developing their understanding of the rational number system and strengthening their use of tables, graphs, and equations, along with properties of arithmetic, to represent and find solutions to problems. A strong general mathematics course in grade 8, focused on building students' skills in using symbols to represent their mathematical thinking, is essential for increasing these students' readiness for algebra in high school.

Algebraic notation permeates the mathematics that students learn in grade 8 and in later grades. The Focal Points in grade 8 emphasize the analysis and representation of linear functions and solving linear equations in a variety of contexts, including applications involving geometry and data analysis. In particular, students can use such technology as geometry exploration software and graphing tools in these types of applications to expand their experiences with the mathematics. The use of technology "enriches the range and quality of investigations by providing a means of viewing mathematical ideas from multiple perspectives" (NCTM 2000, p. 25). Much attention should be dedicated to building meaning for the algebraic notation used in these applications and for the various procedures that can be used to solve linear equations, with the eventual goal being students' ability to apply these understandings as they engage in the reasoning, sense making, and problem solving expected in high school mathematics and beyond.

The three grade 8 Focal Points and their Connections are reproduced on the following page.

Grade 8 Curriculum Focal Points

Algebra: Analyzing and representing linear functions and solving linear equations and systems of linear equations

Students use linear functions, linear equations, and systems of linear equations to represent, analyze, and solve a variety of problems. They recognize a proportion ($y/x = k$, or $y = kx$) as a special case of a linear equation of the form $y = mx + b$, understanding that the constant of proportionality (k) is the slope and the resulting graph is a line through the origin. Students understand that the slope (m) of a line is a constant rate of change, so if the input, or x-coordinate, changes by a specific amount, a, the output, or y-coordinate, changes by the amount ma. Students translate among verbal, tabular, graphical, and algebraic representations of functions (recognizing that tabular and graphical representations are usually only partial representations), and they describe how such aspects of a function as slope and y-intercept appear in different representations. Students solve systems of two linear equations in two variables and relate the systems to pairs of lines that intersect, are parallel, or are the same line, in the plane. Students use linear equations, systems of linear equations, linear functions, and their understanding of the slope of a line to analyze situations and solve problems.

Geometry and Measurement: Analyzing two- and three-dimensional space and figures by using distance and angle

Students use fundamental facts about distance and angles to describe and analyze figures and situations in two- and three-dimensional space and to solve problems, including those with multiple steps. They prove that particular configurations of lines give rise to similar triangles because of the congruent angles created when a transversal cuts parallel lines. Students apply this reasoning about similar triangles to solve a variety of problems, including those that ask them to find heights and distances. They use facts about the angles that are created when a transversal cuts parallel lines to explain why the sum of the measures of the angles in a triangle is 180 degrees, and they apply this fact about triangles to find unknown measures of angles. Students explain why the Pythagorean theorem is valid by using a variety of methods—for example, by decomposing a square in two different ways. They apply the Pythagorean theorem to find distances between points in the Cartesian coordinate plane to measure lengths and analyze polygons and polyhedra.

Data Analysis and *Number and Operations* and *Algebra:* Analyzing and summarizing data sets

Students use descriptive statistics, including mean, median, and range, to summarize and compare data sets, and they organize and display data to pose and answer questions. They compare the information provided by the mean and the median and investigate the different effects that changes in data values have on these measures of center. They understand that a measure of center alone does not thoroughly describe a data set because very different data sets can share the same measure of center. Students select the mean or the median as the appropriate measure of center for a given purpose.

Connections to the Focal Points

Algebra: Students encounter some nonlinear functions (such as the inverse proportions that they studied in grade 7 as well as basic quadratic and exponential functions) whose rates of change contrast with the constant rate of change of linear functions. They view arithmetic sequences, including those arising from patterns or problems, as linear functions whose inputs are counting numbers. They apply ideas about linear functions to solve problems involving rates such as motion at a constant speed.

Geometry: Given a line in a coordinate plane, students understand that all "slope triangles"—triangles created by a vertical "rise" line segment (showing the change in y), a horizontal "run" line segment (showing the change in x), and a segment of the line itself—are similar. They also understand the relationship of these similar triangles to the constant slope of a line.

Data Analysis: Building on their work in previous grades to organize and display data to pose and answer questions, students now see numerical data as an aggregate, which they can often summarize with one or several numbers. In addition to the median, students determine the 25th and 75th percentiles (1st and 3rd quartiles) to obtain information about the spread of data. They may use box-and-whisker plots to convey this information. Students make scatterplots to display bivariate data, and they informally estimate lines of best fit to make and test conjectures.

Number and Operations: Students use exponents and scientific notation to describe very large and very small numbers. They use square roots when they apply the Pythagorean theorem.

Reprinted from *Curriculum Focal Points for Prekindergarten through Grade 8 Mathematics: A Quest for Coherence* (Reston, Va.: NCTM, 2006, p. 19).

Focusing on Linear Functions and Linear Equations

In grade 8, students learn how to analyze and represent linear functions and solve linear equations and systems of linear equations. They learn how to represent linear relationships as graphs, tables, and equations. Students learn the meaning of slope and y-intercept and how these two elements of the graph of a linear function can be identified in each of three representations of a linear relationship—algebraic, tabular, and graphical. They also gain an understanding of the meaning of linear function and that the algebraic representation of a linear function is a linear equation. The eventual goal of this Focal Point is for students to use their understanding of linear functions and linear equations to represent and solve problems.

Instructional Progression for Linear Functions and Linear Equations

The focus on linear functions and linear equations in grade 8 is supported by a progression of related mathematical ideas before and after grade 8, as shown in table 2.1. To give perspective to the grade 8 work, we first discuss some of the important ideas that students focused on before grade 8 that prepare them for learning about linear functions and linear equations in grade 8. At the end of the detailed discussion of this grade 8 Focal Point, we present examples of how students will use linear functions and linear equations in later grades. For more detailed discussions of the "before" parts of the instructional progression, please see the appropriate grade-level books, for example, *Focus in Grade 6* (NCTM 2010) and *Focus in Grade 7* (NCTM 2010).

Early Foundations for Understanding Linear Functions and Linear Equations

Before entering the grade 8 classroom, students are expected to have learned concepts and skills that they can use to understand their work in linear functions and linear equations. In grade 7, students develop efficient, accurate, and generalizable methods for operating with all rational numbers. They learn to graph and represent proportional relationships. Students also use linear equations in one variable and rational numbers to solve word problems.

Table 2.1

Grade 8: Focusing on Linear Functions and Linear Equations—Instructional Progression for Linear Functions and Linear Equations

Before Grade 8	Grade 8	After Grade 8
Students develop efficient, accurate, and generalizable methods for operating with rational numbers. Students recognize fractions, percents, and certain decimals as ways of representing rational numbers and convert flexibly among fractions, decimals, and percents. Students are able to explain which fractions correspond to terminating decimals. Students graph proportional relationships and recognize the graph as a line through the origin with the constant of proportionality as the slope of the line. Students express proportional relationships as $y = kx$ and distinguish them from other relationships, such as $y = kx + b$. Students use linear equations in one variable to solve word problems.	Students translate among algebraic, geometric (graphical), numerical (tabular), and verbal representations of linear functions. Students recognize the slope of a line as a constant ratio representing the change in y compared with the related change in x. Students recognize the y-intercept of a line as the point $(0, y)$ where the line crosses the y-axis. Students recognize relationships that are functions and develop an understanding of how the algebraic representations of linear functions are linear equations. Students relate systems of equations to pairs of lines that intersect, are parallel, or are the same line in the plane and understand that the solution to a system of equations is a solution to both equations. Students analyze and solve problems using linear equations and systems of linear equations.	Students understand numbers, ways of representing numbers, and relationships among numbers within different number systems (e.g., rationals, reals). Students apply operations appropriately, compute fluently, and make reasonable estimates within different number systems. Students understand relations and functions. Students represent and analyze mathematical situations and structures using algebraic symbols. Students use mathematical models to represent and understand quantitative relationships. Students analyze change in various contexts.

Rational numbers

In grade 7, students learn about the set of rational numbers along with the operations of addition and multiplication, along with their inverses of subtraction and division, as being components of the rational number system. They learn that the set of rational numbers is made up of every number that can be expressed as a/b, where a is an integer and b is an integer other than 0. The set of rational numbers includes the integers, since any integer a can be written as $a/1$. Any nonzero rational number can be expressed as a positive or negative fraction and as a positive or negative decimal that terminates or repeats; zero, although neither positive nor negative, also can be expressed as a fraction and as a terminating decimal. Students explore the properties of the operations in the rational number system, comparing and contrasting the properties of these operations that exist in the system of whole numbers and the system of rational numbers. In their study of the properties of operations, students learn about the concept of closure and how to decide whether an operation in a system is closed. Students also develop computational procedures that they use to add, subtract, multiply, and divide with rational numbers, both positive and negative.

During their study of the rational number system, students develop an understanding of percent as a part-to-whole ratio where *n* percent means *n* parts out of 100 total parts. Students flexibly translate among percent, fraction, and decimal forms. For example, students who know that 76 percent means 76 out of 100 use their understanding of rational numbers and ratio to reason that

$$76\% = 76/100 = 0.76 = 19/25.$$

Proportionality

Students' work with proportionality in grade 7 also prepares them to study linear functions and linear equations in grade 8. In grade 7, students express proportional relationships algebraically as equations of the form $y = kx$, where

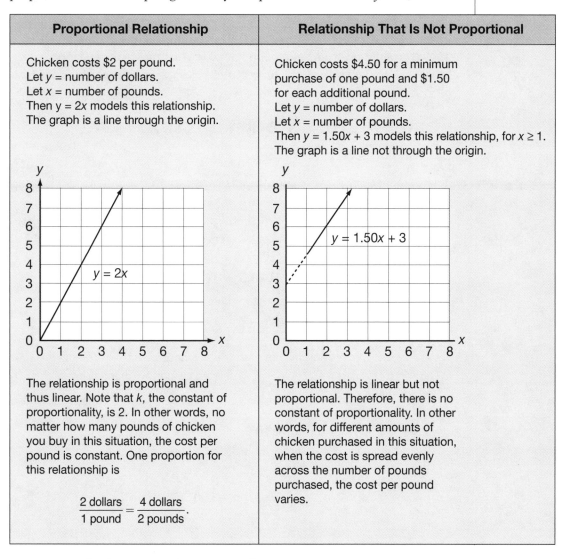

Proportional Relationship	Relationship That Is Not Proportional
Chicken costs $2 per pound. Let y = number of dollars. Let x = number of pounds. Then $y = 2x$ models this relationship. The graph is a line through the origin.	Chicken costs $4.50 for a minimum purchase of one pound and $1.50 for each additional pound. Let y = number of dollars. Let x = number of pounds. Then $y = 1.50x + 3$ models this relationship, for $x \geq 1$. The graph is a line not through the origin.
The relationship is proportional and thus linear. Note that k, the constant of proportionality, is 2. In other words, no matter how many pounds of chicken you buy in this situation, the cost per pound is constant. One proportion for this relationship is $$\frac{2 \text{ dollars}}{1 \text{ pound}} = \frac{4 \text{ dollars}}{2 \text{ pounds}}.$$	The relationship is linear but not proportional. Therefore, there is no constant of proportionality. In other words, for different amounts of chicken purchased in this situation, when the cost is spread evenly across the number of pounds purchased, the cost per pound varies.

Fig. 2.1. Comparing a proportional relationship with a relationship that is not proportional

k is the constant of proportionality. Students also graph these relationships, recognizing the graph as a line through the origin whose slope is k. Students learn to distinguish proportional relationships from relationships that are not proportional, including linear functions whose equations have the form $y = mx + b$, where $b \neq 0$, as shown in figure 2.1.

In grade 8 students apply this understanding as they learn about linear functions and the linear equations that represent them. They learn that $y = mx + b$ is one form of a linear equation and that $y = kx$ represents a linear equation where $m = k$ and $b = 0$. Thus, a proportional relationship between two variables can always be modeled by a linear function, but not all linear functions represent proportional relationships.

Equations

In grade 6 students learn how to represent relationships algebraically using expressions and equations. They learn how to use substitution to evaluate expressions, and they learn various ways to solve equations. They learn that a numerical solution to an equation is a number that makes the equation true. Students also use expressions and equations to solve word problems.

Focusing on Linear Functions and Linear Equations

There are many types of relationships between quantities and many different ways to describe them in order to make predictions and to solve problems. In this Focal Point, students learn about linear relationships and how to use words, graphs, tables, and equations to represent them, as shown in figure 2.2.

Representations of linear relationships

In previous grades, students learn about equations and use equations in one variable to solve problems. For example to solve the problem

> Ed works in a restaurant. He earns $8 per hour plus tips. One day he earned a total of $83, including $35 from tips. How many hours did he work that day?

students have written and solved the equation as follows:

$$8x + 35 = 83$$
$$8x + 35 - 35 = 83 - 35$$
$$8x = 48$$
$$\frac{8x}{8} = \frac{48}{8}$$
$$x = 6$$

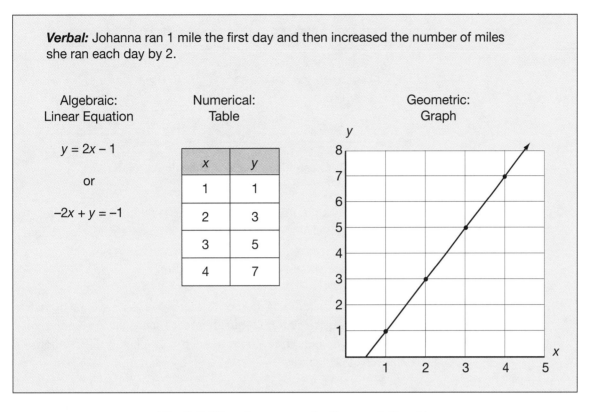

Verbal: Johanna ran 1 mile the first day and then increased the number of miles she ran each day by 2.

| Algebraic: Linear Equation | Numerical: Table | Geometric: Graph |

$y = 2x - 1$

or

$-2x + y = -1$

x	y
1	1
2	3
3	5
4	7

Fig. 2.2. Ways to represent a linear relationship

They have discussed that there is only one solution to this equation, $x = 6$, and that the solution, in the context of the problem, means that Ed worked six hours that day.

In grade 8, students expand their understanding of equations to include linear equations in two variables. A linear equation is an algebraic equation in which each term is either a constant or the product of a constant (called a *coefficient*) and the first power of a single variable. Some linear and nonlinear equations are shown in figure 2.3.

Linear equations in two variables are used to describe the relationship between two quantities. For example, in the equation $y = 2x$, the quantity y is two times the quantity x. In the equation $y = x + 5$, the quantity y is five more than the quantity x. Teachers can help students make the transition from linear equations in one variable to linear equations in two variables by giving them appropriate contextual situations to model, as shown in the following classroom discussion.

Teacher: Here is the problem we were working on solving by using an equation:

Linear Equations	Nonlinear Equations
$x - 3 = 7$ or $x^1 - 3 = 7$	$x^2 - 3 = 7$
$2x - y = 12$ or $2x^1 - y^1 = 12$	$2x^2 - y = 12$
$c = a + b$	$xy = 1$
$3 + x = y - 7$	$\dfrac{1}{x} = y + 3$

Fig. 2.3. Examples of linear and nonlinear equations

This weekend Rick did homework for 6 hours. He did homework for twice as long as he played soccer. How many hours did Rick play soccer?

Who would like to share their equation and solution?

Maddie: I would. Rick did his homework for twice as long as he played soccer. He did his homework for 6 hours. So, I let *s* stand for the number of hours he played soccer and wrote the equation 6 = 2*s*. Then, I divided both sides by 2 to solve the equation:

$$6 = 2s$$
$$\frac{6}{2} = \frac{2s}{2}$$
$$3 = s$$

I got *s* = 3, so Rick played soccer for three hours. This makes sense because 6 = 2(3) is true.

Teacher: The equation that Maddie wrote involves one variable, *s*. There is one solution to this equation. The solution for the equation is 3 = *s*, and so the solution set is one value for *s*. Suppose I changed the situation to—

This weekend Rick did homework and played soccer. He did homework for twice as long as he played soccer.

In this context, you don't know how long Rick did homework or played soccer, but you do know something about the relationship between the amount of time he spent doing each activity. We can use an equation to represent this relationship. Let's use *h* to represent the time that Rick did homework and *s* to represent the time that Rick played soccer. Who can tell me an equation that you can write to represent this relationship?

Shaundra: I think I can. Rick did homework twice as long as he played soccer, so the time spent on homework is 2 times the time spent on soccer, or

$h = 2s$. This is almost the same as Maddie's equation, except I used h for the homework and Maddie used 6.

Teacher: Equations such as $h = 2s$ are linear equations that involve two variables and are used to show the relationship between two quantities, in this case the relationship between the number of hours spent doing homework, h, and the number of hours playing soccer, s. A line on the coordinate plane represents the solutions to this equation. Notice that the solution to the one-variable equation, $6 = 2s$, is related to the point on the line $h = 2s$ where $h = 6$ and $s = 3$.

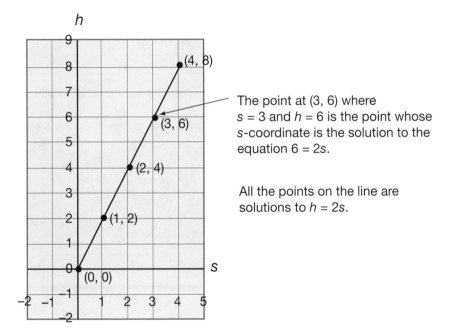

The point at (3, 6) where $s = 3$ and $h = 6$ is the point whose s-coordinate is the solution to the equation $6 = 2s$.

All the points on the line are solutions to $h = 2s$.

Teachers could then change the situation to show that if they change the relationship between the number of hours spent doing homework and the number of hours spent playing soccer, the equation that represents that relationship changes as well, as shown in figure 2.4.

For students to understand how equations can be used to represent the relationship between quantities, they also need to learn about solution sets to these equations. A solution to an equation in two variables is an ordered pair of values that makes the equation true. For example, in the equation $y = 2x$, a solution is an ordered pair in the form (x, y). There are infinitely many solutions to this equation, with a few shown in figure 2.5.

As students have learned in their previous work with coordinate graphing, the order of the numbers in an ordered pair is very important. Teachers can further emphasize this concept by having students analyze equations and their solutions in context. For example, if, in the equation $y = 2x$, x is the

Let x represent number of hours spent playing soccer; let y represent number of hours spent doing homework.

$y = 2x$ ← Rick spends twice as many hours doing homework as he does playing soccer.

$y = x + 3$ ← Rick spends 3 more hours doing homework than he does playing soccer.

$x = 4$ ← Rick spends 4 hours playing soccer regardless of the amount of time he spends doing homework.

$y = 5$ ← Rick spends 5 hours doing homework regardless of the amount of time he spends playing soccer.

Fig. 2.4. Different equations that represent different relationships

$(1, 2)$ is a solution to the equation $y = 2x$	$(35, 70)$ is a solution to the equation $y = 2x$	$(-5, -10)$ is a solution to the equation $y = 2x$	$\left(-\dfrac{2}{3}, -1\dfrac{1}{3}\right)$ is a solution to the equation $y = 2x$
because—	because—	because—	because—
$y = 2x$ $2 = 2(1)$ $2 = 2$	$y = 2x$ $70 = 2(35)$ $70 = 70$	$y = 2x$ $-10 = 2(-5)$ $-10 = -10$	$y = 2x$ $-1\dfrac{1}{3} = 2\left(-\dfrac{2}{3}\right)$ $-1\dfrac{1}{3} = -\dfrac{4}{3} = -1\dfrac{1}{3}$

Fig. 2.5. Using substitution to demonstrate that several ordered pairs are solutions to the equation given

number of people and y is the number of books, the ordered pair $(2, 4)$ represents two people and four books; however, the ordered pair $(4, 2)$ represents four people and two books. If the relationship is that every person has two books, the ordered pair $(4, 2)$ would *not* be a solution for that equation.

Linear equations are so named because the graphical representation of a linear equation is a line in the coordinate plane. Students can see that this is true as they connect the solutions of two variable linear equations with what they already know about graphing in the coordinate plane. Students learn that since every ordered pair corresponds to a point in a coordinate plane, a set of ordered pairs can be graphed. To generate this set of ordered pairs, students can choose values for x or y, substitute those values in the equation, and solve for the other variable. The resulting values form an ordered pair that is a solution to the equation. Students may find it helpful to organize these values in a table, as shown in figure 2.6.

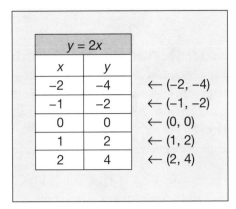

y = 2x	
x	y
−2	−4
−1	−2
0	0
1	2
2	4

← (−2, −4)
← (−1, −2)
← (0, 0)
← (1, 2)
← (2, 4)

Fig. 2.6. Using a table to display ordered pairs that are solutions to the equation y = 2x

Students can then use their understanding of graphing points in the coordinate plane to use the ordered pairs to make a graph, as shown in figure 2.7.

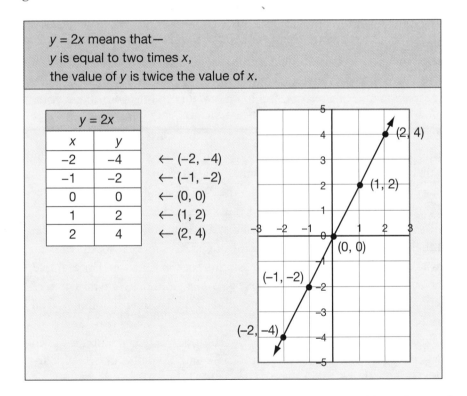

y = 2x means that—

y is equal to two times x,

the value of y is twice the value of x.

y = 2x	
x	y
−2	−4
−1	−2
0	0
1	2
2	4

← (−2, −4)
← (−1, −2)
← (0, 0)
← (1, 2)
← (2, 4)

Fig. 2.7. Showing solutions to the equation y = 2x using a table and a graph

Reflect As You Read

Before reading the next paragraph, articulate for yourself why it is important for students to understand the different possible representations of a linear relationship: a verbal description, a numerical description (a table or set of ordered pairs), a geometrical description (a graph), and an algebraic description (an equation). What are the strengths of each representation?

Each of the four representations of a linear relationship that appear in figure 2.7—a verbal description, a numerical description (a table or set of ordered pairs), a geometrical description (a graph), and an algebraic description (an equation)—has advantages, helping students understand the relationship in a different way. A verbal representation can be more effective for communicating an idea and confirming an understanding. For example, when students can say that $y = 2x$ means the value of y is twice the value of x, they are confirming that they understand the relationship. A table of ordered pairs shows more of the actual numerical information from the situation being represented. An equation is a more concise form of the numerical relationship between the quantities; for example, $y = 2x$ is more concise than *the value of y is twice the value of x*. An equation also concisely and completely summarizes all the ordered pairs in the relationship and can be manipulated algebraically to be written in different, equivalent forms that are useful for different purposes. A graph of a relationship is a representation that provides a visual "picture" of the relationship. In particular, the graph of a linear equation illustrates two attributes of the linear function that are especially significant—slope (indicating the steepness of the line and the direction of its slant or whether it is horizontal or vertical) and the y-intercept (indicating where it intersects the y-axis). Students deepen their understanding of linear relationships by building connections among these various representations.

As students study linear relationships, it is beneficial for linear functions and their equations to be introduced in context. Context allows students to draw accurate conclusions about the solutions of the equation. For example, if the equation $y = 2x$ is considered out of context and there are no stated restrictions on the values of the variables, then x can be any real number. And if x can be any real number in this equation, then y can be any real number that can be described as $2x$. So the number of solutions to the equation is infinite. The graph also reflects these properties. The graph is a line, drawn with arrows at each end indicating that the line extends in both directions without end and with no "holes," indicating that every point on that line is a solution to the equation. Thus, (1.3, 2.6), (2, 4), and (–16, –32) are all solutions to the equation and represent points on the line. However, if the equation is considered in context—for example, it describes the relationship between the number of books and the number of people—then certain solutions make sense and certain solutions do not. Since books and people are not fractional, only whole-number solutions make sense. This illustrates the fact that equations and graphs are representations of functions that can be used to *model* actual situations. In many actual situations, the values for the variables must be restricted. Although the graph shown in figure 2.7 shows the solution to the equation $y = 2x$, not every point on that line is the solution to a problem in which the number of books is two times the number of people.

Once students understand how to graph linear equations, they should revisit previous linear relationships that they have represented using equations. Referring back to figure 2.4, students can now gain a deeper understanding of the representations of the possible relationships between the time Rick spent doing homework and the time he spent playing soccer. Each equation is different, so each graph is different, as shown in figure 2.8.

Let x represent number of hours spent playing soccer; let y represent number of hours spent doing homework.

$y = 2x$ Rick spends twice as many hours doing homework as he does playing soccer.

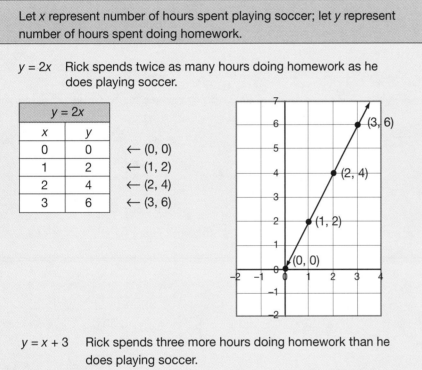

$y = 2x$	
x	y
0	0
1	2
2	4
3	6

← (0, 0)
← (1, 2)
← (2, 4)
← (3, 6)

$y = x + 3$ Rick spends three more hours doing homework than he does playing soccer.

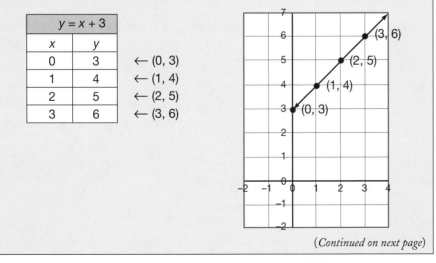

$y = x + 3$	
x	y
0	3
1	4
2	5
3	6

← (0, 3)
← (1, 4)
← (2, 5)
← (3, 6)

(Continued on next page)

Fig. 2.8. Graphs of linear equations

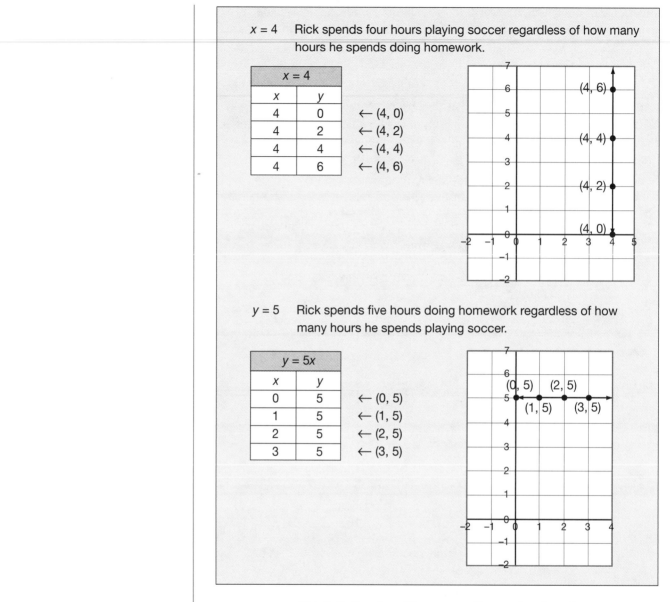

$x = 4$ Rick spends four hours playing soccer regardless of how many hours he spends doing homework.

x = 4	
x	y
4	0
4	2
4	4
4	6

← (4, 0)
← (4, 2)
← (4, 4)
← (4, 6)

$y = 5$ Rick spends five hours doing homework regardless of how many hours he spends playing soccer.

y = 5x	
x	y
0	5
1	5
2	5
3	5

← (0, 5)
← (1, 5)
← (2, 5)
← (3, 5)

Fig. 2.8. Graphs of linear equations—*Continued*

Note that some linear equations are written with only one variable. Students can see from graphs like the ones in figure 2.8 that the graph of an equation of the form $x = a$ is a vertical line and the graph of an equation of the form $y = b$ is a horizontal line, where a and b can be different constants for given equations. Note also that when considering ordered pairs as solutions, there can be many solutions for one-variable equations just as there can be many solutions for two-variable equations.

Slope and *y*-intercept

To develop a deep understanding of linear equations and linear functions, it is important for students to understand how different mathematical relationships between two quantities are reflected in the graph of the line that represents those relationships. A graph provides a "picture" of the relationship, and students can deepen their understanding of linear relationships by building connections between certain mathematical relationships reflected in the equation and certain characteristics that are reflected in the corresponding graph. Through structured experiences in which students make comparisons between purposefully chosen equations and their corresponding graphs, students learn that characteristics of the graphs, such as slope and y-intercept, are affected by changing the mathematical relationships between the two quantities, that is, by changing the relationship between x and y. Students also learn how to use generalizations to describe those changes; for example, when the linear relationship is expressed as $y = mx + b$, the greater the absolute value of the coefficient of x, the steeper the slope, and the greater the number added to mx, the greater the value of y at which the line intersects the y-axis. Through carefully structured opportunities for comparison, students gain the ability to visualize the corresponding graph when they see an equation in the form $y = mx + b$ (i.e., How steep is the line? Does y increase or decrease from right to left? Where does it cross the y-axis?); and to write the corresponding equation when they see the graph of a line (i.e., What are the values for m and b?)

Slope

In initial experiences with exploring the relationship between linear equations and their graphs, teachers should begin with an equation such as $y = x$ in context. In this equation, the value of the two quantities is equal. Teachers should help students connect this relationship to their work with proportionality by pointing out that this equation represents a proportional relationship, $y = kx$, with a constant of proportionality of 1. Then, as teachers change the equation by changing the constant of proportionality, students examine how the change affects the graph. The following classroom discussion illustrates how these comparisons can be accomplished. If available, the use of graphing technology can further enhance students' explorations since it will allow students to create, compare, and analyze many graphs quickly, accurately, and efficiently.

Teacher: Suppose you and your friend always read the same number of pages of a book in one day. Let x represent the number of pages your friend reads; let y represent the number of pages you read. What equation represents the relationship between the pages that you read and the pages that your friend reads?

Josh: $y = x$, because I read the same number of pages as my friend, so x and y have the same value.

Teacher: That equation does represent the situation. So if you read seven pages, your friend reads seven pages. If you read sixteen pages, your friend reads sixteen pages, and so on. How can you use a graph to show this equation?

Tam: Usually I make a table of x- and y-values, and then I use those pairs of values to plot points on the coordinate grid. But since $y = x$, the ordered pairs have the same x- and y-values, so I can just choose any numbers. I chose $(2, 2), (4, 4), (5, 5), (7, 7)$, and $(10, 10)$. My graph looks like this:

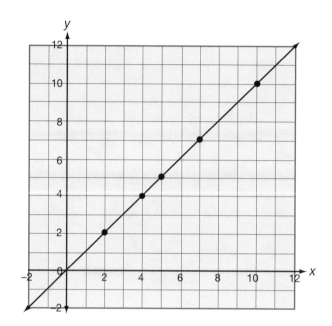

Teacher: Tam remembered that the solution set of the equation $y = x$ is the set of all ordered pairs (x, y) that make the equation true. Tam's ordered pairs reflect a few solutions in the solution set. Notice that the points seem to lie in a straight path. It is true that all these points lie on the same line, and we'll learn more about why later. Did anyone else use different points and make a different graph?

Ned: I used $(0, 0), (1, 1), (2, 2), (3, 3)$, but my graph looks just like Tam's. It looks like a line and has the same slant and passes through the origin.

Teacher: Interesting observations, Ned. What Ned observed is that regardless of which ordered pairs that solve the equation you choose to use to graph the equation $y = x$, all the ordered pairs fall on the same straight line. Did anyone use negative values to graph the line?

Matt: I like negative numbers, so I used $(-2, -2)$ and $(-1, -1)$. But I realized that you can't really read a negative number of pages, so I guess my ordered pairs don't make much sense in the problem!

Teacher: Good point, Matt. The equation $y = x$ is a model of the relationship between the pages you read and the pages your friend reads per day. Although all the points that fall on the straight path of the line are solutions to the equation, not all make sense in the context of the problem. Would the solution (1 1/4, 1 1/4) make sense?

Matt: I think so, because you can read a fractional number of pages. I guess my friend and I could both read 1 1/4 pages of a book. But greater numbers, like 2000, wouldn't make sense.

Once students understand the solutions to the equation and what they mean in the context of the problem, and how the graph shows the relationship in the problem, they are ready to begin gaining an understanding of how changing the equation changes the graph, as illustrated in the continuation of the classroom discussion that follows.

Teacher: Now suppose every day you read twice as many pages as your friend reads. What equation would you use to represent that relationship?

Shakira: Well, if I still use *y* as the number of pages I read and *x* as the number of pages that my friend reads, my equation would be *y* = 2*x*, meaning I read twice as many pages as my friend.

Teacher: How can you graph this equation?

Shakira: I would make a table of *x*- and *y*-values to find ordered pairs to graph. My table and graph look like this:

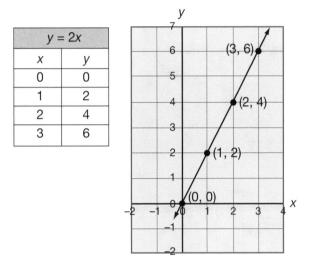

Teacher: Now let's compare the graph of *y* = *x* and the graph of *y* = 2*x*. It is much easier for us to compare graphs when they are on the same scale, so why don't we just graph them on the same coordinate grid. Who can describe some similarities and some differences in the two graphs?

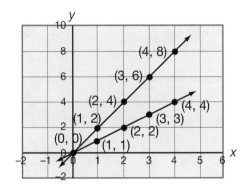

Harry: Well, they are both straight lines, and they both pass through the origin.

Kira: But look, the graph of the line for $y = 2x$ is steeper than the graph of the line for $y = x$.

Teachers should then have students look at the graphs separately and draw triangles as shown in figure 2.9. Students should begin to gain an awareness that, although the triangles look different in the two graphs, all the triangles in one graph are similar to one another and all the triangles in the other graph are similar to one another; that is, their corresponding sides are proportional and their corresponding angles are congruent. This characteristic not only justifies that the points in each graph all lie on a straight line but also can be used to describe the slant of each line.

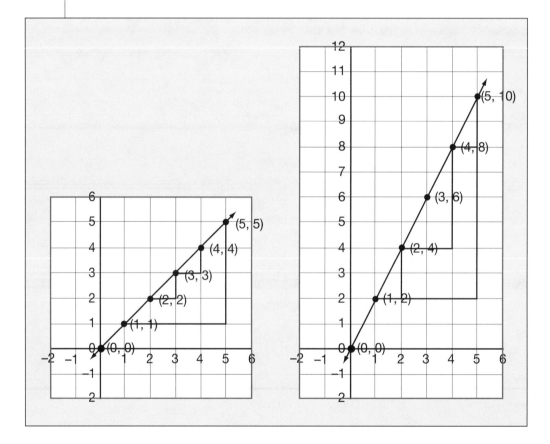

Fig. 2.9. Examples of how similar right triangles are formed by pairs of points on a line

Teachers should then extend students' experiences with graphs by introducing graphs with negative slope, that is, where k is negative, as shown in the continuation of the class discussion that follows.

Teacher: So far, we've considered only situations that involve a constant increase. We also can create equations that model situations that involve a constant decrease. For example, suppose I want to represent a situation where the temperature is dropping 3 degrees every hour. I could write the equation $y = -3x$. In this equation, x represents the number of hours that have elapsed and *y* represents the total change in temperature over that amount of time. Let's graph this equation.

Bruce: I made a table of values and then used that table to find ordered pairs. Then I graphed the ordered pairs. The line in quadrant II stands for the time before I started recording the temperature. This is what my table and graph look like:

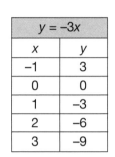

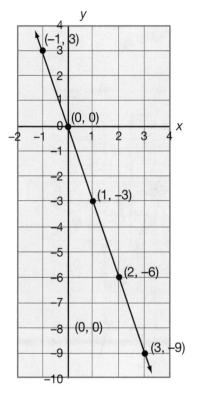

Teacher: How is this line graph different from all the other lines you have made?

Hillary: It still goes through the origin, but it goes down. All the other lines went up.

Teacher: Usually we think of a graph as changing from left to right, or as the value of *x* is increasing. So when we look from left to right on this graph, this line is descending; all the other lines "went up," or were ascending, as the value of *x* increased. That makes me want to look at the equation $y = -3x$ and think about how it is different from the other equations.

Jack: It has a negative number times *x*; all the other ones had a positive number times *x*.

Teacher: Yes, all our equations have been in the form $y = mx$, so we can compare them. In this equation, the coefficient of *x* is a negative number, $m = -3$. Since *m* describes the slope, the slope of this line is negative. This seems to indicate that an equation with a negative slope is a descending line. The equations that we have seen with positive slopes all had ascending lines. Let's look at more lines.

Teachers should then have students explore other relationships represented by an equation in the form $y = kx$, including equations in which k is negative, and analyze how the changes in the relationship represented by the equation affect the graph, as shown in figure 2.10. Through carefully crafted experiences, students should be able to start making generalizations about $y = kx$, such as the greater the absolute value of k, the steeper the line; when k is positive, the graph is a line that rises from left to right; when k is negative, the graph is a line that falls from left to right; and all equations in the form $y = kx$ pass through the origin.

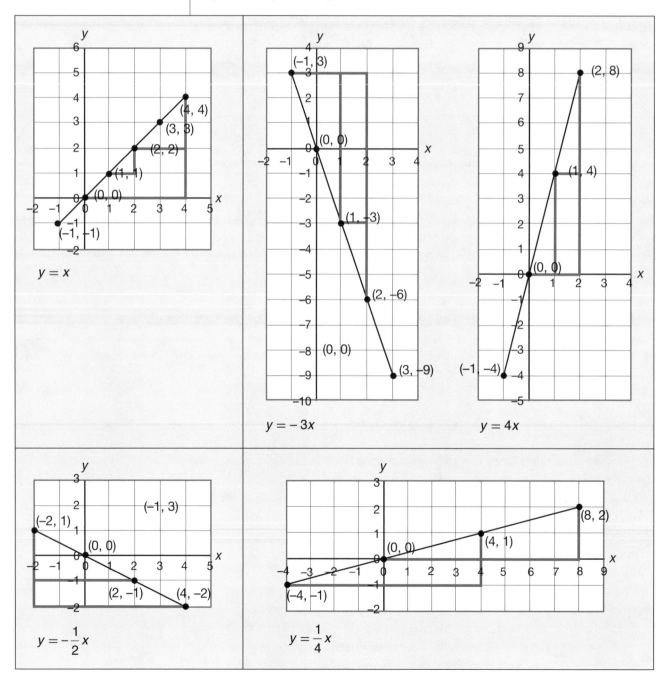

Fig. 2.10. Comparing the graphs of different equations in the form $y = kx$

After students have begun to gain the ability to generalize about the steepness and direction of the slant of the line given the equation, teachers can help students link their previous understanding of proportionality and slope to linear equations. Teachers should remind students that the equation $y = x$ represents a proportional relationship in the form $y = kx$ in which the constant of proportionality, k, is 1. Students should be guided to make the transition from thinking of k as the constant of proportionality to thinking of it as the slope of the line represented by the equation. For example, in the equation $y = x$, $k = 1$, so the slope is 1. Classroom discussions such as the one that follows can help students accomplish this connection of what they understand about proportionality with their developing understanding of slope.

Teacher: We have compared equations and their corresponding graphs and have discovered that the steepness of the line is related to the constant k in the equation $y = kx$. If we kept the scale the same, we saw that the steeper the line, the greater the absolute value of k. When k was a number whose absolute value was between 0 and 1, the line became more and more horizontal as the absolute value of k lessened. The "slant" or "tilt" of a line is also called its *slope*. Does anyone remember how slope is defined mathematically?

Charra: I think I remember that. It is a ratio, right? A ratio of the change in y to the change in x.

Teacher: Yes, Charra, that is the definition of the slope of a line. We can write slope as the ratio

$$\frac{\text{change in } y\text{-value}}{\text{change in } x\text{-value}}.$$

And for any two points on a line, this ratio is a constant value. We can use this ratio to find the slope of any line. Let's look back at some of the graphs that we made, for example, the graph of the line for the equation $y = x$. To find the slope, choose two points on the line, for example B at $(4, 4)$ and C at $(5, 5)$. Then write a ratio of the difference between the y-values to the difference between the x-values:

$$\frac{5-4}{5-4} = \frac{1}{1} = 1.$$

The ratio is equal to 1, so the slope of the line is equal to 1. Notice that this relationship is true no matter which two points you choose on the line. For each pair of points, the ratio of the change in y-values to the change in corresponding x-values is 1.

Timmy: That makes sense because those triangles are supposed to be similar, which means that their corresponding sides are proportional.

Teachers can use diagrams like the one shown in figure 2.11 to help students visualize and verify mathematically how slope indicates the constant rate of change in a line. Teachers should point out that the triangles that are formed by the line and a segment that represents the change in *y*-values and a segment that represents the change in corresponding *x*-values are all similar; therefore any two points on a line can be used to calculate its slope.

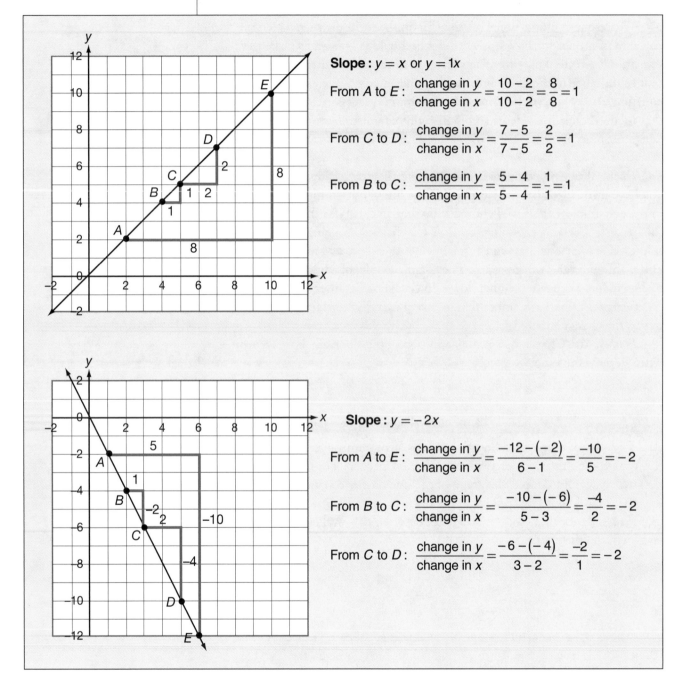

Slope: $y = x$ or $y = 1x$

From *A* to *E*: $\dfrac{\text{change in } y}{\text{change in } x} = \dfrac{10 - 2}{10 - 2} = \dfrac{8}{8} = 1$

From *C* to *D*: $\dfrac{\text{change in } y}{\text{change in } x} = \dfrac{7 - 5}{7 - 5} = \dfrac{2}{2} = 1$

From *B* to *C*: $\dfrac{\text{change in } y}{\text{change in } x} = \dfrac{5 - 4}{5 - 4} = \dfrac{1}{1} = 1$

Slope: $y = -2x$

From *A* to *E*: $\dfrac{\text{change in } y}{\text{change in } x} = \dfrac{-12 - (-2)}{6 - 1} = \dfrac{-10}{5} = -2$

From *B* to *C*: $\dfrac{\text{change in } y}{\text{change in } x} = \dfrac{-10 - (-6)}{5 - 3} = \dfrac{-4}{2} = -2$

From *C* to *D*: $\dfrac{\text{change in } y}{\text{change in } x} = \dfrac{-6 - (-4)}{3 - 2} = \dfrac{-2}{1} = -2$

Fig. 2.11. Diagram that shows slope as the ratio of the change in *y*-values to the change in corresponding *x*-values

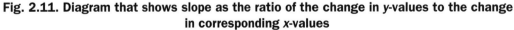

Teachers should then have students revisit previous graphs to find their slopes by finding the ratio of the change in y to the change in x for several pairs of points on the line, points not only with integral coordinates but also with coordinates involving fractions and decimals. Through these experiences, students should be able to generalize that when a line is ascending, both the change in x and the change in y are positive, and so the slope is positive. However, when a graph is descending, either the change in x or the change in y is negative and the other change is positive, which results in a negative slope.

At this point, students should have enough experiences with finding the slope of lines that represent equations that they can conclude that in the equation $y = kx$, k is the slope. Students are then ready to make the transition from using the symbols $y = kx$ to using $y = mx$, where m represents the slope, thus integrating their understanding of proportionality and slope, that is, that the constant of proportionality (also called the *scale factor*) in a proportional relationship is the slope of the graph of that relationship. Throughout their work with linear equations and graphing, students should be reminded that the equation $y = mx$ is the same equation they used to represent a proportional relationship, just with the symbol m in place of the symbol k. Referring back to figure 2.11, students can see that in the graph of $y = x$ or $y = 1x$, for every 1-unit change in y up, there is a 1-unit change in x to the right, so the slope is 1; in the graph of $y = -2x$, for every -2-unit change in y down, there is a 1-unit change in x to the right so, the slope is -2.

During explorations of slope, teachers can guide students to an algebraic representation of the slope by helping them realize that given two points on the line (x_1, y_1) and (x_2, y_2), the slope is found by finding the ratio of the difference of the y-values, $(y_2 - y_1)$, to the difference of the corresponding x-values, $(x_2 - x_1)$. This ratio can be written as the fraction

$$\frac{(y_2 - y_1)}{(x_2 - x_1)}.$$

Teachers can explain that the change in y is also called the *rise* and the change in x is called the *run*, so

$$\textbf{slope} = m\frac{(y_2 - y_1)}{(x_2 - x_1)} = \frac{\text{rise}}{\text{run}}.$$

The tables in figure 2.12 illustrate this relationship between the differences in the y-values compared to the differences in the x-values.

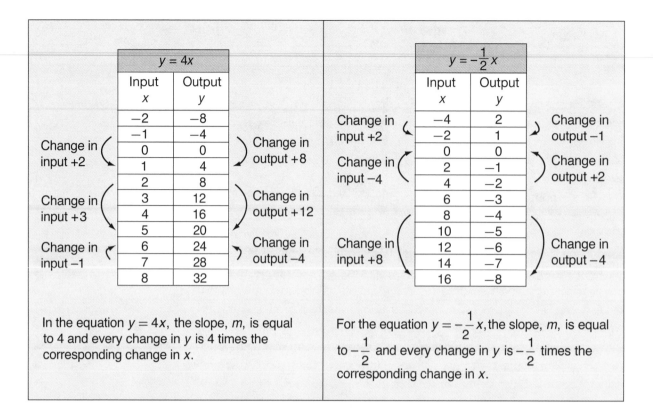

Fig. 2.12. Examples that show that if the input changes by *a*, then the output changes by *ma*, where *m* is the slope

During their exploration of graphing equations, students should also have experience graphing equations in which the slope is 0 or the slope is undefined. Students' explorations of the linear equations $y = a$ and $x = b$, where a and b are rational numbers, can help them understand these special cases of linear equations—equations that have only one variable—as shown in figure 2.13.

As students work through examples such as $y = 1$, $y = -2$, and $y = 0$ (the *x*-axis) and $x = 2$, $x = -5$, and $x = 0$ (the *y*-axis), they can begin to see that every horizontal line has a slope of zero and an equation of the form $y = b$, where b is a constant, and that the equation for a vertical line is an equation of the form $x = a$, where a is a constant, and that slope is not defined for vertical lines.

y-intercept

Through their work with graphing equations of the form $y = mx$, students gain an intuitive understanding of how the constant of proportionality, *m*, or the slope, affects the steepness of a line. Given the equation, they can determine how steep the line will be and whether it will be ascending, descending, vertical, or horizontal. Another important aspect that students need to consider when trying to visualize the line that represents a linear equation is where the line crosses the *y*-axis. The point at which the line crosses the *y*-axis is called the *y*-intercept. Students learn that if they can identify the slope

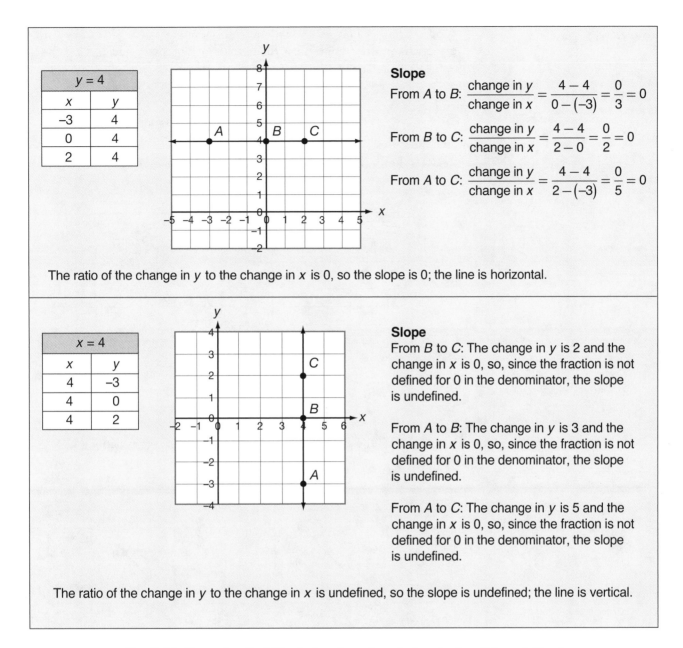

Fig. 2.13. Examples that illustrate when slope is 0 and when it is undefined

and the *y*-intercept, they have all the information necessary to visualize and, if they wish, draw the graph.

In students' initial explorations of linear equations and their graphs, they have considered equations in the form *y* = *mx*. As students mature in their understanding, they begin to explore equations in the form *y* = *mx* + *b*. Teachers can continue to build on students' understanding of linear equations and their graphs, as shown in the following classroom discussion.

Teacher: Remember that we used the equation *y* = *x* to model the situation in which you read the same number of pages every day that your friend reads. Now let's change that situation a bit. Suppose you read one more page every day than your friend. If y is the number of pages you read and x is the number of pages your friend reads, what equation shows the relationship?

Timmy: $y = x + 1$. So, if my friend reads nine pages, I read ten. If my friend reads fifteen pages, I read sixteen, and so on.

Teacher: That equation does model the problem. Who can show us how to graph it?

Maria: I can. My table of values and graph look like this:

 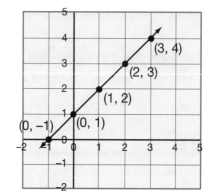

Teacher: We have been comparing many graphs. Let's compare the graph of $y = x + 1$ with the graph of $y = x$. Tell me about some similarities and differences.

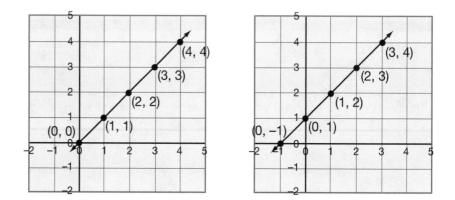

Maria: The slopes are the same, but $y = x$ passes through the origin and $y = x + 1$ passes through the y-axis at $(0, 1)$ and the x axis at $(-1, 0)$.

Teacher: Those are interesting observations, Maria. Let's look at some other pairs of graphs.

Teachers should then have students explore related pairs of equations and graphs, such as those shown in figure 2.14. Having students graph pairs of equations on the same coordinate plane can help them more easily identify similarities and differences. Teachers can have students verify the value of the *y*-intercept by substituting 0 for *x*, because the *x*-coordinate of the *y*-intercept is 0, and solving the equation for *y*. This is useful to help students see that, for example, the *y*-intercept of the graph of $y = (1/3)x - 5$ is –5.

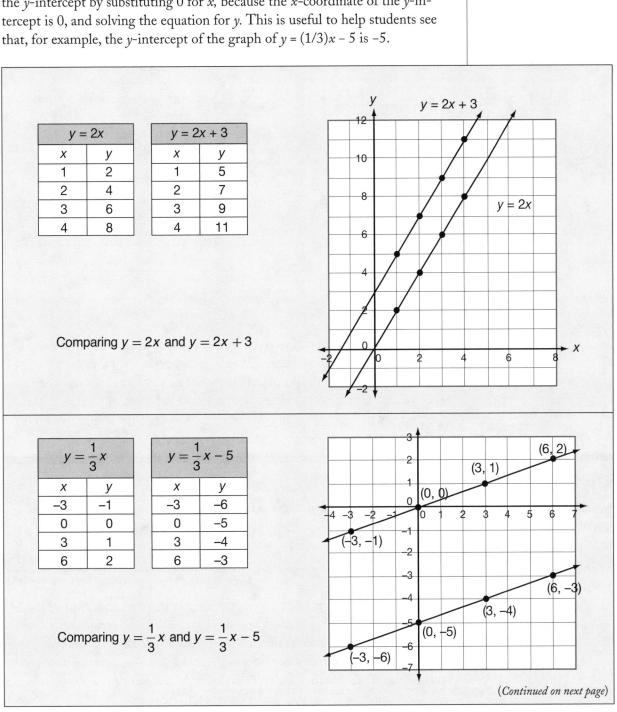

Comparing $y = 2x$ and $y = 2x + 3$

$y = 2x$	
x	y
1	2
2	4
3	6
4	8

$y = 2x + 3$	
x	y
1	5
2	7
3	9
4	11

$y = \dfrac{1}{3}x$	
x	y
–3	–1
0	0
3	1
6	2

$y = \dfrac{1}{3}x - 5$	
x	y
–3	–6
0	–5
3	–4
6	–3

Comparing $y = \dfrac{1}{3}x$ and $y = \dfrac{1}{3}x - 5$

(*Continued on next page*)

Fig. 2.14. Comparing pairs of related graphs

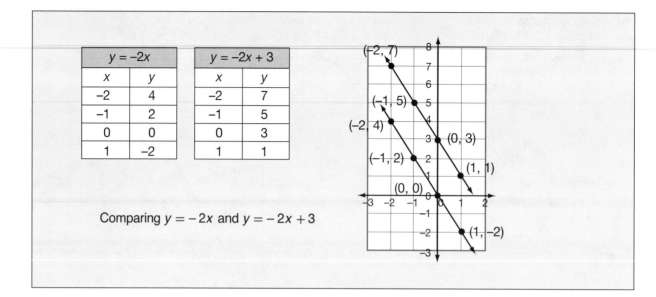

y = −2x	
x	y
−2	4
−1	2
0	0
1	−2

y = −2x + 3	
x	y
−2	7
−1	5
0	3
1	1

Comparing $y = -2x$ and $y = -2x + 3$

Fig. 2.14. Comparing pairs of related graphs—*Continued*

As students are guided to compare pairs of graphs such as the ones in figure 2.14, they might conjecture that in an equation in the form $y = mx + b$, b is the y-coordinate of the point at which the line crosses the y-axis. They may also realize that when the slope is the same and the value of b changes, the steepness of the corresponding line stays the same but the line moves up or down the y-axis.

Reflect As You Read

What is the ultimate goal of having students do activities in which they explore linear equations, slopes, and y-intercepts? What prior background do your students bring to this discussion that you can build on?

After students have had many opportunities to graph equations of the form $y = mx + b$, teachers should explain that the slope-intercept form of a linear equation is $y = mx + b$, where m is the slope and b is the y-intercept. This is called the slope-intercept form and can be used to describe any non-vertical linear relationship. (A vertical line is described by $x = a$, where a is a constant.) The slope, m, and the y-intercept, b, are the numbers that tell you the relationship between all of the x-y pairs that describe the points on the line, and if you change the slope or y-intercept, you change the relationship. The corresponding tables and graphs change as well.

At this point, students can strengthen their understanding of the connection between proportionality and linear equations, that is, that the proportional relationship, $y/x = k$, or $y = kx$, is a special case of a linear equation in the form $y = mx + b$, where $m = k$ and $b = 0$ and, since b, the y-intercept, is equal to 0, the corresponding lines cross the y-axis at (0, 0), the origin. Also, students should realize that the equation $y = x$ can be written in the form $y = mx + b$ as $y = 1x + 0$, where the slope is 1 and the y-intercept is 0.

The ultimate goal of activities exploring linear equations, slopes, and y-intercepts is to help students begin to gain the ability to visualize the graph of an equation—to gain a sense of how steep the line is, where it is in relation to the axes on the coordinate plane, and whether it rises or falls. After teachers have guided students through carefully crafted examples such as the ones previously described, students, when given $y = 4x - 5$ for example, should be able to articulate that the slope can be described by "over 1, up 4" or "up 4, over 1" and be able to create a mental picture of about how steep that is in relation to the scale used in the graph. In addition, students should realize that the graph of the line crosses the y-axis at –5 and be able to picture about where that is on the coordinate plane. Also, if students are given two lines, for example one represented by $y = 4x - 5$ and one represented by $y = 3x - 5$, they should be able to visualize and explain in what ways these lines are the same and different, that is, that the line representing $y = 4x - 5$ is a little steeper than the line representing $y = 3x - 5$ and that they cross the y-axis at the same point, (0, –5).

Once students have gained these understandings, they will have developed skills necessary to identify the slope and y-intercept by looking at an equation in slope-intercept form or at the graph of a line. They will also have the skills necessary to graph a line given an equation in slope-intercept form as well as write an equation in slope-intercept form given the graph of a line. Students should be prepared to complete activities such as those shown in figure 2.15.

Problem 1:
What are the slope and y-intercept of the line related to the equation $y = 3x - 4$? Use the slope and y-intercept to graph the equation.

Solution:
$y = 3x - 4$: Because the constant ratio of change in y to change in x is that for every change of 1 in x, there is a change in y of 3 (to the right 1, up 3), the slope is 3/1 = 3; and the y-intercept is –4, so the graph crosses the y-axis at (0, –4).

Graph:

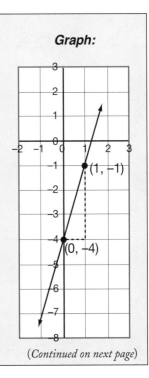

(*Continued on next page*)

Fig. 2.15. Problems showing relationships among y-intercept, slope, equations, and lines

Problem 2:
Look at the graph. What are the slope and *y*-intercept? Use the slope and *y*-intercept to write an equation in slope-intercept form that the graph represents.

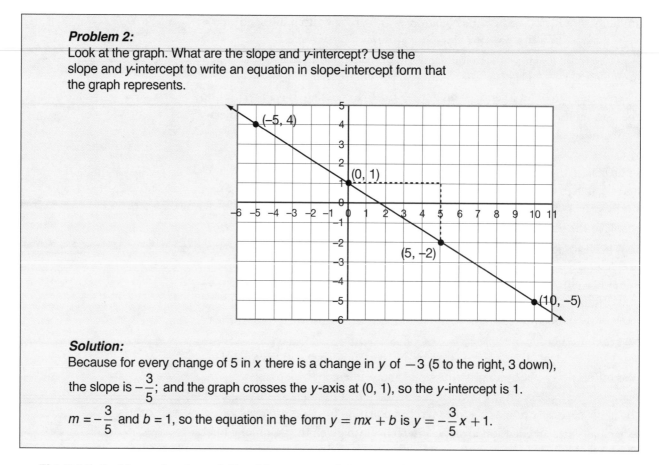

Solution:
Because for every change of 5 in *x* there is a change in *y* of −3 (5 to the right, 3 down),

the slope is $-\frac{3}{5}$; and the graph crosses the *y*-axis at (0, 1), so the *y*-intercept is 1.

$m = -\frac{3}{5}$ and $b = 1$, so the equation in the form $y = mx + b$ is $y = -\frac{3}{5}x + 1$.

Fig. 2.15. Problems showing relationships among *y*-intercept, slope, equations, and lines—*Continued*

Relations and functions

Students' study of linear equations is part of the study of the larger concept of functions, which stems from a discussion of relations. In grade 8, students learn that a relation is a set of ordered pairs and that a function is a relation in which each input (or *x*-value) has exactly one output (or *y*-value). Some relations are functions and some are not, and some relations can be described by a nice compact equation, and some cannot, as illustrated in figures 2.16, 2.17, and 2.18.

Team members' ages and heights	
Input *a* Age (years)	Output *h* Height (inches)
14	66
14	64
15	68
14	65
13	60

This relation is not a function because there is an input paired with more than one output.

The input 14 has three different outputs.

Fig. 2.16. A relation that is not a function

Earnings	
Input *h* Hours worked	Output *p* Pay (dollars)
1	4
3	12
5	20

This relation is a function because each input is paired with exactly one output.

The input function can be described by the rule $p = 4h$.

Fig. 2.17. A relation that is a function that can be described by a compact, symbolic rule

Basketball team		
Player's last name	Input *x* Alphabetical position	Output *y* Jersey number
Ames	1	10
Beck	2	31
Evans	3	25
Graff	4	12
Johnson	5	13
Rios	6	14
Turner	7	33
Wells	8	22

This relation is a function because each input is paired with exactly one output.

There is no compact, symbolic rule for this function.

Fig. 2.18. A relation that is a function that cannot be described by a compact, symbolic rule

The rule for the earnings function in figure 2.17 is $p = 4h$, and the ordered pairs (h, p) are (1, 4), (3, 12), and (5, 20). In this function the values of one variable depend on the values of the other variable. For example, it makes sense to say that p, the amount of pay, depends on h, the number of hours worked. So we say that h is the independent variable and p is the dependent variable. Because a dependent/independent relationship exists in many functions, the first variable in the ordered pairs is often called independent, the second variable is called dependent, and the rule is stated as an equation in terms of the independent variable. When the function is graphed, convention dictates that we usually use the horizontal axis for the independent variable and the vertical axis for the dependent variable.

In their study of functions, students learn that some functions are linear and some are not. If a function is linear, it can be represented by a linear equation and its graph is a line. If a function is nonlinear, any rule, or equation, that may be able to be written to represent the function is *not* a linear equation and the graph of the equation is not a line. For example, the area of a square can be represented as a function of the length of a side of the square ($A = s^2$), and this relationship results in a graph that is not a line, as shown in figure 2.19.

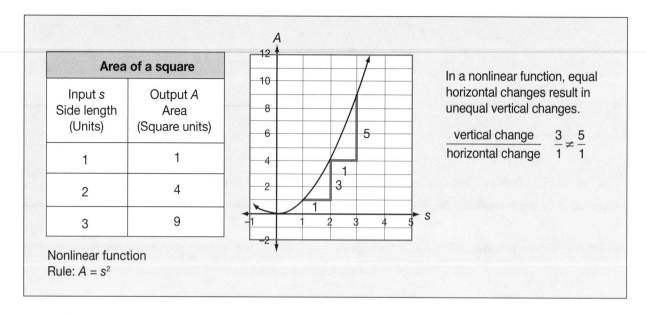

Area of a square	
Input s Side length (Units)	Output A Area (Square units)
1	1
2	4
3	9

Nonlinear function
Rule: $A = s^2$

In a nonlinear function, equal horizontal changes result in unequal vertical changes.

$$\frac{\text{vertical change}}{\text{horizontal change}} \quad \frac{3}{1} \neq \frac{5}{1}$$

Fig. 2.19. Unequal ratios of horizontal and vertical changes in a nonlinear function

Important properties of linear equations and linear functions are summarized in figure 2.20.

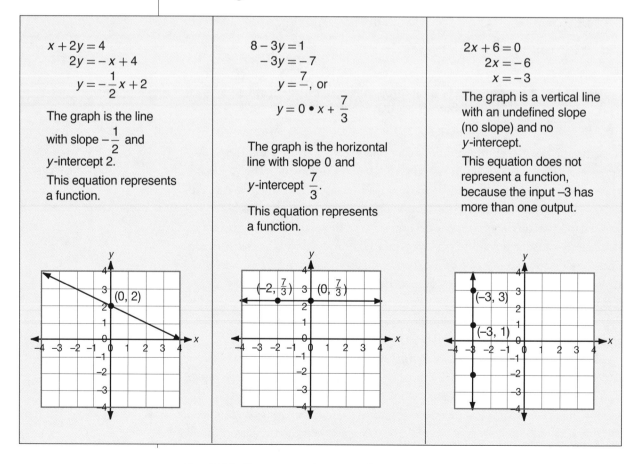

$x + 2y = 4$
$2y = -x + 4$
$y = -\dfrac{1}{2}x + 2$

The graph is the line with slope $-\dfrac{1}{2}$ and y-intercept 2.

This equation represents a function.

$8 - 3y = 1$
$-3y = -7$
$y = \dfrac{7}{3}$, or
$y = 0 \bullet x + \dfrac{7}{3}$

The graph is the horizontal line with slope 0 and y-intercept $\dfrac{7}{3}$.

This equation represents a function.

$2x + 6 = 0$
$2x = -6$
$x = -3$

The graph is a vertical line with an undefined slope (no slope) and no y-intercept.

This equation does not represent a function, because the input –3 has more than one output.

Fig. 2.20. Linear equations and linear functions

Systems of linear equations

Students apply their understanding of linear equations as they begin to investigate systems of equations. In their work with equations, they learn that a system of linear equations in two variables is a set of two or more linear equations that contain one or both of those two variables. In grade 8, the focus of the work with systems of equations is for students to understand the meaning of "a solution to the system." At this level, students' work will mostly involve numerical and graphical representations of solutions, although in later grades they will explore systems and their solutions algebraically. To begin this exploration, students' work may be limited to systems of equations whose solutions are ordered pairs of integers, to more easily locate the point of intersection, simplify computation, and focus on the meaning of "finding a solution to a system of linear equations." Students' exploration of systems of linear equations can be broadened to more complex situations if they are given the opportunity to use graphing technology in their explorations.

As with students' initial work with equations, students should begin exploring systems of equations in context. Understanding the meaning of the solution to a system of equations in the context of a problem is an essential component in students' developing their competence with systems of linear equations. Teachers can help students begin to build this understanding through classroom discussions such as the following:

Teacher: Let's think about this problem.

Suppose you want to join an online music site. Site A charges $6.00 per month plus $1.25 for each song you download. Site B charges $2.00 for each song you download and has no monthly fee. How many songs would you have to download in one month to make the costs of the sites the same?

The work we have been doing with linear equations and graphing can help you solve this problem. First, we can write an equation to represent the cost of participating in site A for one month. Barb, how might we do that?

Barb: Well, in site A, there is a $6 a month charge plus $1.25 charge for each song you download. So I would write the equation $y = 1.25x + 6$, where x is the number of songs you download and y is the total charge for one month.

Teacher: That equation does represent the cost of songs for a month at site A. Now, can someone provide an equation for participating in site B for one month?

Jeremy: Site B has no monthly fee, but the cost of downloading each song is higher; it is $2 for each song, so $y = 2x$, where x is the number of songs downloaded in a month and y is the total cost.

Teacher: Let's look at the question "How many songs would you have to download in one month to make the cost of both sites the same?" along with our equations: $y = 1.25x + 6$ and $y = 2x$. These equations have the same variables, x and y. We call equations with the same variables a system of equations. The question asks us how many songs you would have to download in one month to make the cost of the sites the same. In both equations the number of songs is represented by x and the total cost is represented by y. One way to think about the problem is that we can write solutions to each equation as ordered pairs (x, y) and that the question asks us to find the specific ordered pair (x, y) that is a solution to both equations. One way to find this ordered pair is to graph the equations. Take a few minutes to sketch a graph of $y = 1.25x + 6$. [The teacher gives students time to work.] Who would like to share with us what they did?

Gerry: I made a table of values that solved the equation and then used the ordered pairs to make the graph of the line that goes with the equation. My table and graph look like this:

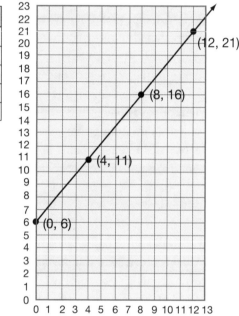

$y = 1.25x + 6$	
x	y
0	6
4	11
8	16
12	21

Teacher: That graph does represent the equation. Remember how we graphed equations on the same coordinate plane when we wanted to compare them? Let's try that with these equations. Take a few minutes to graph the second equation on the same coordinate plane. [Pause.] Who can tell me how they graphed $y = 2x$ and what the graph looks like?

Jeremy: I used the slope and the y-intercept to graph $y = 2x$. Since $b = 0$ in the equation, the graph passes through the origin. The slope is 2. I know that the slope is the change in y-values over the change in x-values. So if

$$\text{slope} = 2 = \frac{2}{1},$$

for every change of 1 in the x-values, there is a change of 2 in the y-values. I can use that to graph my line. I put a point at the origin. Then I counted to the right 1 and up 2 and put another point. From there I counted to the right 1 and up 2. Then I did that a third time. Then I drew a line to connect the points. My graph looks like this:

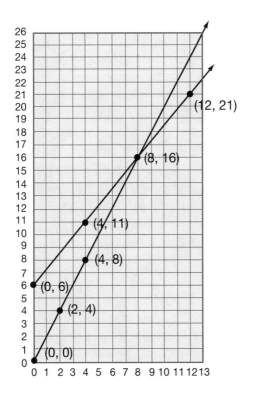

Teacher: Let's compare these graphs. What do you notice?

John: I see that their slopes are different. That makes sense because the value of *m* in the equations is different; in $y = 1.25x + 6$, $m = 1.25$ and in $y = 2x$, $m = 2$.

Barb: I see that where they intersect the *y*-axis is different: $y = 1.25x + 6$ intersects the *y*-axis at (0, 6), and $y = 2x$ intersects at the origin. That makes sense because the *b*-value in $y = 1.25x + 6$ is 6 and in $y = 2x$ it is 0.

Teacher: Is there anything else you notice about the lines?

Gerry: I see that they intersect at a point—at point (8, 16).

Teacher: Interesting observation, Gerry. How did you know that point was (8, 16)?

Gerry: Because the coordinates of the point have to satisfy both equations, and

$$y = 1.25x + 6$$
$$16 = 1.25(8) + 6$$
$$16 = 10 + 6$$
$$16 = 16$$

and

$$y = 2x$$
$$16 = 2(8)$$
$$16 = 16.$$

We might have been sloppy when we drew the graph, so I made sure the numbers worked.

Chantelle: And when I used my graphing calculator to trace to the point where the graphs met, the coordinates said (8, 16).

Teacher: So we can justify that these are the coordinates of the point of intersection. What does (8, 16) mean in the context of the equation for site A?

Gerry: It means that if you download eight songs, the total cost is $16.

Teacher: What does (8, 16) mean in the context of the equation for site B?

Jeremy: It means the same thing! If you download eight songs, the total cost is $16.

Teacher: Remember we said that the question asks us to find the ordered pair (x, y) that is a solution to both equations. The point of intersection shows the point that makes both equations true, so that point is the solution to both equations. In this case, the graphs intersect at (8, 16), so (8, 16) is the solution to the system of linear equations. What does this solution mean in the context of the problem?

Beni: Well, the answer to the problem is eight songs, because if you download eight songs in one month at either place, it will cost you $16 for that month.

Students should explore many problems in which they write and graph pairs of equations within contexts. They should learn that, in general, in a system of two linear equations, the point at which the graphs of those two equations intersect is the solution to the system of equations. Experiences should be carefully structured to include equations that represent parallel lines and equations that are equivalent, so that students can begin to understand the relationships between these types of pairs of equations. For example, two equations involving the same slope are representing either two lines that are parallel and do not intersect or are different equations representing the same line. Therefore, a system of linear equations consisting of equations involving the same slope either does not have a solution or has infinitely many solutions. Students should understand how this makes sense in the context of the problem. For example, referring back to the song download problem, if site A charges $6.00 per month plus $1.25 for each song you download and site B charges $4.00 per month plus $1.25, the cost of downloading songs at site A will always be $2 more than the cost of downloading songs at site B, so the cost will never be the same. Students will see this reflected in the equations and graphs that represent the problems. The equations $y = 1.25x + 6$ and $y = 1.25x + 4$ have the same slope and therefore result in parallel lines. Parallel lines do not intersect, so there is no solution. Graphing equivalent linear equations results in a graph of one line, so all points on the line are solutions to a system consisting of two equivalent equations. After many opportunities to explore a wide variety of purposefully crafted systems of two linear equations, students learn that these systems can have exactly one solution, no solution, or an infinite number of solutions, as illustrated in figure 2.21.

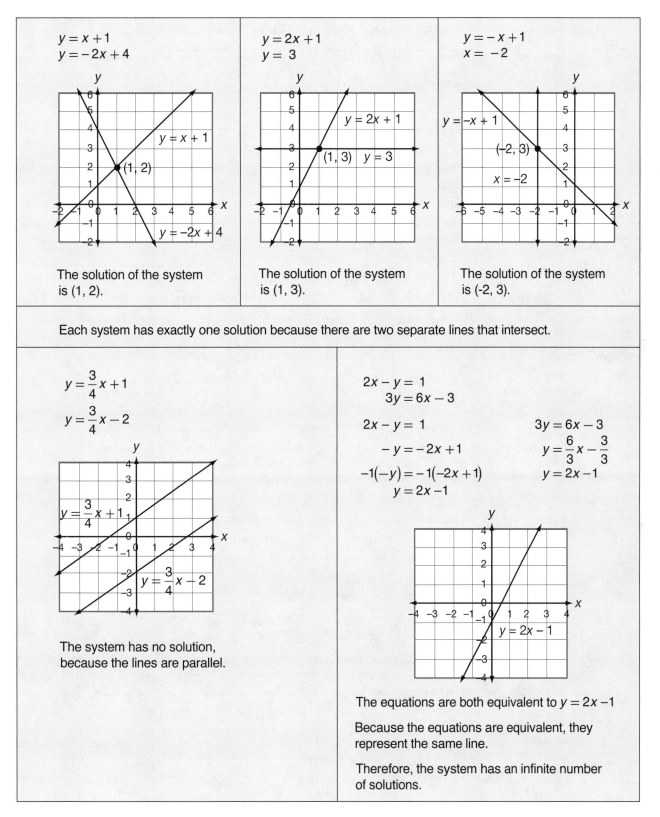

$y = x + 1$
$y = -2x + 4$

The solution of the system is (1, 2).

$y = 2x + 1$
$y = 3$

The solution of the system is (1, 3).

$y = -x + 1$
$x = -2$

The solution of the system is (-2, 3).

Each system has exactly one solution because there are two separate lines that intersect.

$y = \dfrac{3}{4}x + 1$

$y = \dfrac{3}{4}x - 2$

The system has no solution, because the lines are parallel.

$2x - y = 1$
$3y = 6x - 3$

$2x - y = 1$

$\qquad -y = -2x + 1$

$-1(-y) = -1(-2x + 1)$

$\qquad y = 2x - 1$

$3y = 6x - 3$

$y = \dfrac{6}{3}x - \dfrac{3}{3}$

$y = 2x - 1$

The equations are both equivalent to $y = 2x - 1$

Because the equations are equivalent, they represent the same line.

Therefore, the system has an infinite number of solutions.

Fig. 2.21. Different types of solution sets for a system of two linear equations

Focusing on Linear Functions and Linear Equations through Problem Solving

Students' understanding of linear functions and linear equations deepens as they solve problems involving functional relationships that are linear. Students can use their skills to write equations and create graphs that help them model and solve these problems. Throughout students' problem-solving experiences, teachers should be sure that students understand what the x- and y-values and slope of a line mean in the context of the problem. Students should also be reminded that although all the points on a line are solutions to the linear equation, they may not all make sense as solutions in the context of the problem. For example, suppose Matthew always plays his trumpet fifteen minutes longer than he plays his clarinet. The equation $t = c + 15$ can be used to describe the time Matthew plays his trumpet. The point $(-13, 2)$ on the line is related to the equation because

$$t = c + 15$$
$$2 = (-13) + 15$$
$$2 = 2$$

However, it doesn't make sense that Matthew would spend -13 minutes playing his clarinet, so the solution does not make sense in the context of the problem. In the case of this situation, only nonnegative solutions would make sense. In many real-life situations, like this one, only the solutions on the c axis and in the first quadrant of the coordinate plane make sense.

Teachers should give students a variety of problems in which they write and graph equations to find solutions. One such problem is shown in figure 2.22.

Problem:

To train for a bicycle race, you ride from your house to a park that has a loop trail. It takes you 1 minute to ride to the park, $1\frac{1}{2}$ minutes to ride each lap of the trail, and 1 more minute to ride home. Let y represent the total number of minutes it takes you to ride to the park, ride x laps of the trail, and then ride back home. How many minutes will it take to ride to the park, ride 6 laps, and then ride home? Explain how you can use an equation and a graph to find the answer.

Solution:

You can write the equation $y = \frac{3}{2}x + 2$ to represent the relationship between total time and number of laps. If you ride 6 laps, then $x = 6$, and you can solve for y to find the total time:

(*Continued on next page*)

Fig. 2.22. Example that shows how to use a linear equation and a graph to solve a problem

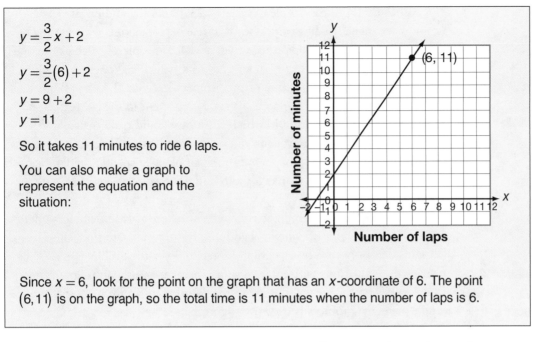

$y = \dfrac{3}{2}x + 2$

$y = \dfrac{3}{2}(6) + 2$

$y = 9 + 2$

$y = 11$

So it takes 11 minutes to ride 6 laps.

You can also make a graph to represent the equation and the situation:

Since $x = 6$, look for the point on the graph that has an x-coordinate of 6. The point $(6, 11)$ is on the graph, so the total time is 11 minutes when the number of laps is 6.

Fig. 2.22. Example that shows how to use a linear equation and a graph to solve a problem—*Continued*

Teachers should be sure to include problems in which students can extend the line of the graph to find the solution to the problem, such as the one shown in figure 2.23.

Problem:
You are selling drinks at a school play to earn money for the drama club. The graph shows how the profit is related to the number of drinks you sell. How many drinks do you need to sell to earn a $30 profit? A $40 profit?

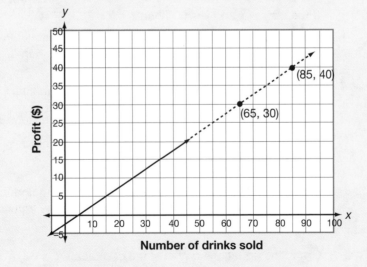

Solution:
You can extend the graph to find the answers. The line crosses the point (65, 30) and (85, 40), so you need to sell 65 drinks to make a profit of $30 and 85 drinks to make a profit of $40.

Fig. 2.23. Example of extending a graph to solve a problem

Notice that in the example in figure 2.23, fractional and negative values do have meaning. It is important that teachers include a wide variety of problems in which the slope is negative, as well as problems, such as the one in figure 2.23, in which fractional and negative values make sense. Teachers can extend students' exploration of the problem in figure 2.23 by asking such questions as "What does the point (0, –5/2) represent in the context of the problem? Explain a situation in which this point could make sense." (–5/2 is equal to a loss of $2.50. This solution means that if you sell no drinks, you will lose $2.50. This could happen if, for example, you spend $2.50 on ice and you can return all unsold drinks for a refund, then you will lose $2.50 if you sell no drinks.)

Teachers should also include rich and varied problems in which students need to write systems of equations and graph the systems to find solutions. If students do not have access to graphing technology, the problems should be restricted to equations with integral solutions, as it is difficult to graph fractional values precisely enough to read the coordinates from the graph. An example of such a problem is shown in figure 2.24.

Problem:
Students, parents, and teachers are on an eighth-grade field trip. Sixty of them go in a museum. The ticket prices are $2 per student and $4 per adult. The total cost for the tickets is $140. How many adults and how many students bought tickets?

Possible Solution:
Step 1: Write equations to model the problem. Let *x* represent the number of student tickets bought and *y* represent the number of adult tickets bought.

- If the sum of *x* and *y* is 60, then $x + y = 60$.

- If the student tickets are $2 each, then 2*x* represents the total cost of student tickets. If the adult tickets are $4 each, then 4*y* represents the total cost of adult tickets.

- If the total cost of all the tickets is $140, then the sum of the cost of the student tickets and the adult tickets is $140, or
  $2x + 4y = 140$.

- So the system of equations that models the problem is
  $x + y = 60$, and $2x + 4y = 140$.

Step 2: Either write the equations in *y*-intercept form and find the slopes and *y*-intercepts, or find ordered pairs that satisfy the equations as they are written.

Step 3: Graph the equations on the same coordinate plane.

(*Continued on next page*)

Fig. 2.24. Example of using a system of equations to solve a problem

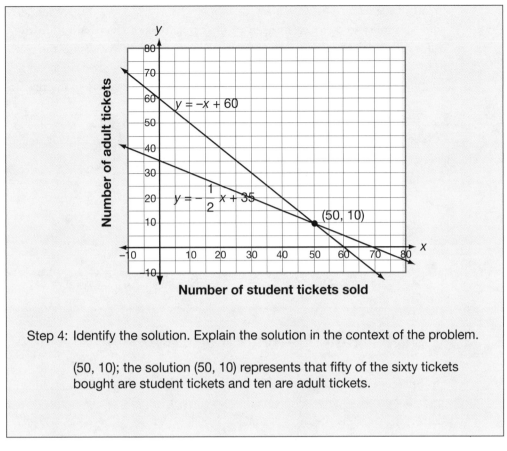

Step 4: Identify the solution. Explain the solution in the context of the problem.

(50, 10); the solution (50, 10) represents that fifty of the sixty tickets bought are student tickets and ten are adult tickets.

Fig. 2.24. Example of using a system of equations to solve a problem—*Continued*

Problems like the one in figure 2.24 can be modified to provide opportunities for deeper understanding of linear equations as models of certain types of situations. Teachers can adjust the numbers in the problem to highlight different information. For example, if the total number of tickets is changed to thirty-one, the ticket prices are \$2 per student and \$5 per adult, and the total cost is \$80, students would write the following equations:

$$x + y = 31$$
$$2x + 5y = 80$$

and the solution would then be (25, 6).

Strengthening Understanding through Connections

In grade 8 students apply their developing understanding of functions as they encounter nonlinear functions, including inverse proportionality and basic quadratic and exponential functions; examine arithmetic sequences; and solve problems involving rates such as motion at a constant speed. Students learn that inverse proportionality (inverse variation) can be modeled by an equation in any of the forms $y = k/x$, $x = k/y$, or $xy = k$, where x, y, and $k \neq 0$. Students gain the ability to contrast inversely proportional relationships with (directly) proportional relationships in the form $y = kx$, $y/x = k$, or $k = y/x$. One example of inverse proportionality that students might encounter involves the possible lengths and widths of a rectangle that has a given area, as shown in figure 2.25.

Possible lengths and widths of a rectangle that has an area of 48 square units:

length x	2	6	8	10	30
width y	24	8	6	4.8	1.6

This inversely proportional relationship can be modeled by the equations

$$y = \frac{48}{x}, x = \frac{48}{y}, \text{ or } xy = 48.$$

Fig. 2.25. Example showing an inversely proportional relationship

Students also encounter basic quadratic and exponential functions in grade 8. For example, students might encounter the quadratic equation $h = 16t^2$, which models the total distance traveled by a free-falling object over time, where h is the number of feet an object falls (neglecting air resistance) in t seconds. An exponential function, $y = 20{,}000(0.85^x)$, is a model for the value of a car that is purchased for $20,000 and decreases in value 15 percent per year, where y represents the value in dollars x years after the purchase. Through their work with linear and nonlinear functions, students learn to recognize that if the rate of change of a function is constant, then the function is a linear function whose graph is a line. However, if the rate of change is not constant, then the function is a nonlinear function whose graph is not a line. The rate of change in the nonlinear function $y = 20{,}000(0.85^x)$ is not constant. Students learn to recognize this nonconstant rate of change as reflected in the table of values for the equation as well as in the nonlinear graph that represents the equation, as shown in figure 2.26.

Students also apply their understanding of linear functions as they deepen their understanding of arithmetic sequences, including those that arise from patterns and problem-solving situations. In grade 6, students learn to connect formulas with sequences. In grade 8, students extend this knowledge as they learn that some of these sequences can be represented as linear functions. For example: If you start with twenty-five music CDs and you buy two new CDs at some time during each month, then the total number of CDs you have at the end of each month is given by the arithmetic sequence below.

| month number | 1, | 2, | 3, | 4, ... (term number in the sequence) |
| number of CDs | 27, | 29, | 31, | 33, ... (term of the sequence) |

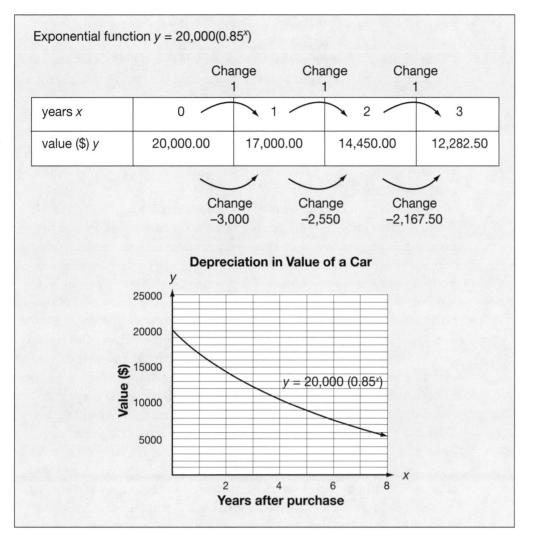

Exponential function $y = 20,000(0.85^x)$

	Change 1		Change 1		Change 1	
years x	0	1	2	3
value (\$) y	20,000.00	17,000.00	14,450.00	12,282.50
	Change −3,000	Change −2,550	Change −2,167.50

Depreciation in Value of a Car

$y = 20,000 (0.85^x)$

Fig. 2.26. Nonconstant rate of change as reflected in a table of values and a graph

This sequence can be represented by the linear function $y = 2x + 25$, where x is the month number and y is the number of CDs.

Students also apply their work with linear equations as they solve problems involving rates. For example, if you are 400 miles from home and you travel toward home at a constant rate of 55 miles per hour, you can model the situation with the equation $y = -55x + 400$, where y represents your distance from home when x hours have elapsed.

Connections in later grades

In later grades students will expand their understanding of number systems. They will learn about different ways of representing numbers, will compute and make reasonable estimates within both the real number system and the complex number system, and will judge the reasonableness of their results. They will study relationships among number systems, learning that the set of real numbers is made up of rational numbers and irrational numbers, whereas the set of complex numbers is made up of real numbers and imaginary numbers.

Students will study the meanings of operations and how they relate to one another. They will judge the effects of such operations as multiplication, division, and computing powers and roots on the magnitudes of quantities. They will find that some solutions to quadratic equations are complex numbers. For example, the solutions to $x^2 = -9$ are the complex numbers $3i$ and $-3i$. Students will also study vectors and matrices as systems that have some of the properties of the real number system, using such operations as addition and multiplication.

Students expand their ability to use deductive reasoning to prove mathematical statements. For example, to prove the statement that the sum of an even and an odd number is always an odd number, students learn to argue that an even number is a whole number that has a factor of 2, so any even number can be represented by $2m$. An odd number is 1 more than an even number, so any odd number can be represented by $2n + 1$, where m and n represent whole numbers. So $2m + (2n + 1) = (2m + 2n) + 1 = 2(m + n) + 1$. Since $2(m + n)$ is an even number and $2(m + n) + 1$ is one more than an even number, $2(m + n) + 1$ is an odd number, and the sum of an odd number and an even number is always an odd number.

Students will continue their study of relations and functions and use functions to generalize more and more complex patterns. They will deepen their ability to analyze functions as they investigate rates of change, intercepts, zeros, asymptotes, and the behavior of a function's graph in key regions. Students will study properties of classes of functions, including exponential, polynomial, rational, logarithmic, and periodic functions. They will add, subtract, multiply, divide, and compose functions and will find inverses of functions. Students will work with expressions, equations, inequalities, relations, and systems of equations. They will use a variety of symbolic representations, including recursive and parametric equations, for functions and relations.

Developing Depth of Understanding

Why is it important to have students make connections among numerical (tabular), geometric (graphical), and algebraic representations of linear relationships? What activities can you give students to help them build a strong understanding of the characteristics of a linear relationship, for example, how do slope and the y-intercept of a line describe the relationship between the coordinates, x and y, of the points on the line?

3 Focusing on Analyzing Geometric Figures and Space by Using Distance and Angle

In grade 8, students learn how to analyze two- and three-dimensional space and figures by using distance and angle. Students learn how to analyze the angles created when parallel lines are cut by a transversal. They also learn the Pythagorean theorem and its converse and apply them to problem-solving situations. The eventual goal of this Focal Point is for students to use the knowledge they acquire about these concepts to solve problems involving distance and angle in two- and three-dimensional figures.

Instructional Progression for Analyzing Geometric Figures and Space by Using Distance and Angle

The focus on distance and angle in grade 8 is supported by a progression of related mathematical ideas before and after grade 8, as shown in table 3.1. To give perspective to the grade 8 work, we first discuss some of the important ideas that students focus on before grade 8 that prepare them for learning how to analyze geometric figures and space by using distance and angle in grade 8. At the end of the detailed discussion of this grade 8 Focal Point, we present examples of how students will analyze geometric figures and space in later grades. For more detailed discussions of the "before" parts of the instructional progression, please see the appropriate grade-level books, for example, *Focus in Grade 6* (NCTM 2010) and *Focus in Grade 7* (NCTM 2010).

Table 3.1 represents an instructional progression for the conceptual understanding of analyzing geometric figures and space before grade 8, during grade 8, and after grade 8.

Early Foundations for Analyzing Geometric Figures and Space by Using Distance and Angle

Before grade 8 students develop an understanding of similarity as a geometric property in which relationships among lengths within an object are preserved and corresponding lengths of similar objects are proportional. They use this understanding to find lengths in similar figures, find distances on maps, and solve other problems involving similarity, as shown in figure 3.1.

Table 3.1
Grade 8: Focusing on Analyzing Geometric Figures and Space by Using Distance and Angle—Instructional Progression for Analyzing Geometric Figures and Space by Using Distance and Angle

Before Grade 8	Grade 8	After Grade 8
Students develop an understanding of similarity as a geometric relationship in which relationships of lengths within an object are preserved and use scale factors to solve problems, for example, finding lengths in similar figures, distances on maps, and so on. Students use proportionality to understand pi and its use in determining circumference and area of a circle (introduce formulas). Students find the surface areas of prisms and cylinders by decomposing the three-dimensional figure into its two-dimensional components. Students derive and justify the formula for volume of prisms and cylinders (volume = area of base × height) by decomposing the three-dimensional figure into smaller component figures. Students understand and are able to describe the relationship between the scale factor and the areas and volumes of similar figures. Students solve a variety of problems involving area, surface area, circumference of circles, and volume of prisms and cylinders using various strategies.	Students create and critique inductive and deductive arguments concerning situations involving the angles formed when two parallel lines are cut by a transversal. Students understand the relationships among the angles, side lengths, perimeters, areas, and volumes of similar objects and use these relationships to solve problems. Students develop an understanding of the Pythagorean theorem (that is, given a right triangle, then the lengths of the sides have a specific relationship) and its converse (that is, given the specific relationship between the lengths of the sides of a triangle, then the triangle must be a right triangle.) Students apply the Pythagorean theorem and its converse to solve problems.	Students analyze characteristics and properties of two- and three-dimensional geometric figures and develop mathematical arguments about geometric relationships. Students specify locations and describe spatial relationships using coordinate geometry and other representational systems. Students apply transformations and use symmetry to analyze mathematical situations. Students use visualization, spatial reasoning, and geometric modeling to solve problems. Students understand measurable attributes of objects and the units, systems, and processes of measurement. Students apply appropriate techniques, tools, and formulas to determine measurements.

Students also learn that in all circles, the circumference is proportional to the diameter and that the constant ratio of circumference to diameter is π (pi). This fact is represented in the circumference formula, that is,

$$\frac{C}{d} = \frac{\pi}{1}$$
$$C \times 1 = \pi d$$
$$C = \pi d.$$

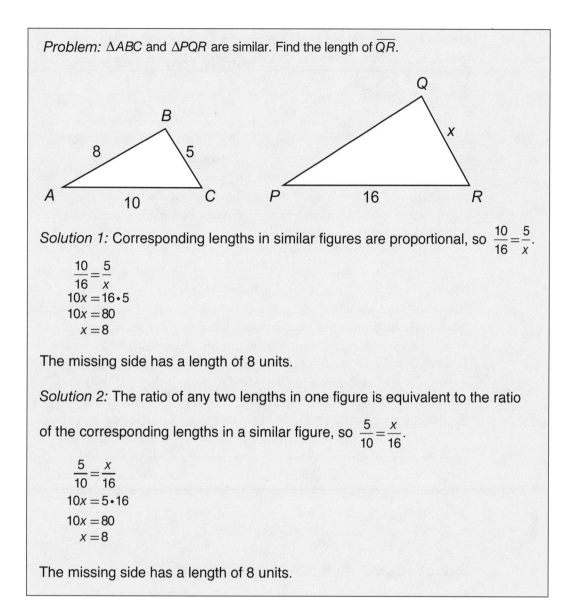

Problem: $\triangle ABC$ and $\triangle PQR$ are similar. Find the length of $\overline{QR}$.

Solution 1: Corresponding lengths in similar figures are proportional, so $\frac{10}{16} = \frac{5}{x}$.

$$\frac{10}{16} = \frac{5}{x}$$
$$10x = 16 \cdot 5$$
$$10x = 80$$
$$x = 8$$

The missing side has a length of 8 units.

Solution 2: The ratio of any two lengths in one figure is equivalent to the ratio

of the corresponding lengths in a similar figure, so $\frac{5}{10} = \frac{x}{16}$.

$$\frac{5}{10} = \frac{x}{16}$$
$$10x = 5 \cdot 16$$
$$10x = 80$$
$$x = 8$$

The missing side has a length of 8 units.

Fig. 3.1. Example showing how to use similarity to solve problems

Students also see an explanation that establishes credibility for the area formula, and they find the diameter, radius, circumference, and area of circles.

In grade 7, students find the surface areas of prisms and cylinders by decomposing three-dimensional figures into their two-dimensional components. They also derive and justify the formula for the volume of prisms and cylinders (volume = area of base × height) by decomposing the three-dimensional figure into smaller component figures. Students understand and are able to describe the relationship between the scale factor and the areas and volumes of similar figures. Students use their understanding of these relevant relationships and formulas along with various strategies to solve a variety of problems involving circumference and area of circles and surface area and volume of prisms and cylinders.

Focusing on Analyzing Geometric Figures and Space by Using Distance and Angle

In grade 8, students use distance and angle to analyze geometric figures and space by developing understandings in three categories: angle relationships formed when parallel lines are cut by a transversal, the Pythagorean theorem, and the relationships that result from similarity. As students work toward attaining these understandings, they use both inductive and deductive reasoning to discover the properties related to distance and angle that are necessary to analyze geometric figures and space.

When teaching geometry in grade 8, it is important to note the existence of Euclidean geometry resulting from a certain set of assumptions, or axioms, and which most of us are familiar with, and non-Euclidean geometries that are results of different sets of assumptions. A basic axiom, or postulate, of Euclidean geometry is the parallel postulate that states, "Given a line and a point not on that line, there is *exactly one* line through the point that is parallel to the line." Two non-Euclidean geometries are hyperbolic geometry and elliptic geometry, each of which has a different parallel postulate from the one in Euclidean geometry and from each other. In hyperbolic geometry there are at least two lines through the point that are parallel to the given line; in elliptic geometry there are no lines through the point that are parallel to the given line. Most, and in many cases all, of the work that students do in geometry is Euclidean geometry until they reach college-level geometry. The concepts in this Focal Point regarding geometric figures and space are concepts of Euclidean geometry. If students were to study corresponding concepts in a non-Euclidean geometry, they would learn some different relationships and results.

Inductive and deductive reasoning

Inductive reasoning is a process of observing a pattern of events or examples and then, on the basis of the pattern, making a conjecture, or unproved conclusion. The conjecture may or may not be true. Inductive reasoning proceeds from the particular to the general. Some examples appear in figure 3.2.

Deductive reasoning is a process of reasoning logically from given facts, using previously established facts and relationships, to reach a conclusion. If the given facts are true and the logic is applied correctly, then the conclusion is true. Deductive reasoning is used in mathematics to prove that a statement is true. This statement is often a conjecture that was created with inductive reasoning. An example of deductive reasoning is shown in figure 3.3.

Once a statement is proved true with deductive reasoning, it is called a *theorem* and can be applied to specific cases; in that way, deductive reasoning can be used to proceed from the general to the particular. For example, after proving that the sum of any two even numbers is even, one can conclude that the sum of 513,256 and 14,808 is an even number without actually doing the calculation.

- Hector sees that the price of a stock increases every month for 10 consecutive months and makes the conjecture that the price will increase in the 11th month.

- Arlo looks at the sequence 3, 5, 8, 12, 17, ... He observes the pattern of the difference between adjacent numbers being 1 more each time and then makes the conjecture that the next number in the sequence is 23.

- Jill examines sums of even numbers, such as 2 + 4 = 6, 4 + 10 = 14, and 18 + 24 = 42, and then makes the conjecture that the sum of any two even numbers is even.

Fig. 3.2. Examples of inductive reasoning

Statement: The sum of any two even numbers is even.

Deductive reasoning to prove the statement:

An even number is a whole number that is divisible by 2, so any even number can be represented by $2n$, where n is a whole number.

Let $2a$ and $2b$ represent any two even numbers, where a and b are whole numbers.

By the distributive property, $2a + 2b = 2(a + b)$.

Because whole numbers are closed with respect to addition, $a + b$ is a whole number.

$2(a + b)$ is even because it is a whole number that is divisible by 2.

Therefore, the sum of any two even numbers is even.

Fig. 3.3. Example of deductive reasoning to prove a statement

Using inductive and deductive reasoning in geometry

Students can use inductive as well as deductive reasoning to explore geometric relationships regarding angle and distance. For example, students can cut apart a triangle, place its angles together, and observe that the angles create a straight line and so have a sum of 180 degrees. If they complete this activity for many different triangles and observe the same result, they can use inductive reasoning to conjecture that the sum of the angles in all triangles is 180 degrees. Also, students can use deductive reasoning in several different ways to prove that the sum of the angles in all triangles is 180 degrees, a statement that can then be used as a theorem. This deductive reasoning involves logical arguments that use definitions, axioms, or existing theorems. An axiom, or postulate, in mathematics is a statement that is accepted as true without proof.

Much of the work that students do in mathematics in kindergarten through grade 8 involves inductive reasoning. Younger students are more able to observe relationships and properties and make conjectures than to use logical reasoning to prove the conjectures. As students advance in mathematics, however, the ability to use deductive reasoning becomes increasingly important. Even in advanced mathematics, though, inductive reasoning still plays an important role. Through inductive reasoning, mathematicians may observe relationships and properties that lead to conjectures that can then be proved or disproved using deductive reasoning.

Angle relationships in intersecting lines

In previous grades students have learned how to measure and classify angles. They have also learned about complementary angles (i.e., angles with measures whose sum is 90 degrees) and supplementary angles (i.e., angles with measures whose sum is 180 degrees) as well as perpendicular and parallel lines. In grade 8 students extend their understanding of angles and their relationships as they learn about vertical angles and their congruence. Students can be guided to use inductive and deductive reasoning as they explore vertical angles, as shown in figure 3.4. Students could also use geometry exploration software as a tool in this activity.

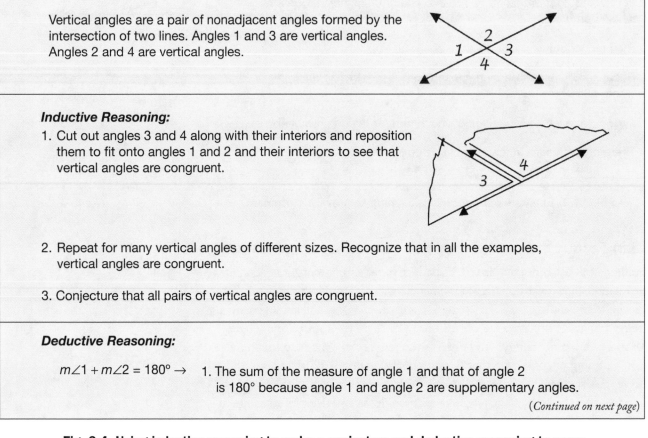

Vertical angles are a pair of nonadjacent angles formed by the intersection of two lines. Angles 1 and 3 are vertical angles. Angles 2 and 4 are vertical angles.

Inductive Reasoning:

1. Cut out angles 3 and 4 along with their interiors and reposition them to fit onto angles 1 and 2 and their interiors to see that vertical angles are congruent.

2. Repeat for many vertical angles of different sizes. Recognize that in all the examples, vertical angles are congruent.

3. Conjecture that all pairs of vertical angles are congruent.

Deductive Reasoning:

$m\angle 1 + m\angle 2 = 180° \rightarrow$ 1. The sum of the measure of angle 1 and that of angle 2 is 180° because angle 1 and angle 2 are supplementary angles.

(Continued on next page)

Fig. 3.4. Using inductive reasoning to make a conjecture and deductive reasoning to prove that vertical angles are congruent

$m\angle 1 + m\angle 2 = 180° \rightarrow$ 2. The sum of the measure of angle 3 and that of angle 2 is 180° because angle 3 and angle 2 are supplementary angles.

$m\angle 1 + m\angle 2 = m\angle 3 + m\angle 2 \rightarrow$ 3. Both sums are equal to 180°.

So, $m\angle 1 = m\angle 3 \rightarrow$ 4. So, because you can subtract the measure of angle 2 from both sides, the measure of angle 1 and the measure of angle 3 are equal to each other.

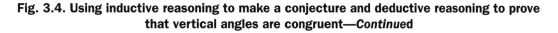

5. Angle 1 and angle 3 represent any pair of vertical angles, so we have proved that all pairs of vertical angles are congruent.

Fig. 3.4. Using inductive reasoning to make a conjecture and deductive reasoning to prove that vertical angles are congruent—*Continued*

Notice that in the deductive reasoning example, students draw on previous knowledge of equations, supplementary angles, and the subtraction property of equality. They connect these ideas to create a logical argument that proves that vertical angles are congruent. Thus, students use prior knowledge in a new way to investigate and understand a new concept.

In grade 8, students use prior knowledge to explore another new concept—the angle relationships formed by the angles created when parallel lines are cut by a transversal. In initial experiences with the transversal diagram, teachers should point out that a *transversal* is a line that crosses two other lines. Different transversal diagrams are shown in figure 3.5.

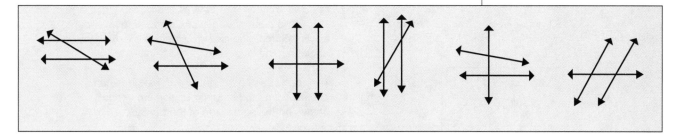

Fig. 3.5. Transversal diagrams

As is illustrated in figure 3.5, a transversal can cross any pair of lines in the same plane; the lines need not be parallel. However, in the transversal diagram involving parallel lines, several interesting angle relationships exist. Before teachers can help students inductively conjecture about and then deductively prove the angle relationships that are formed in a transversal diagram involving parallel lines, students need to understand the vocabulary associated with the angles in a transversal diagram, as shown in figure 3.6. Notice that this vocabulary is the same even if the lines are not parallel.

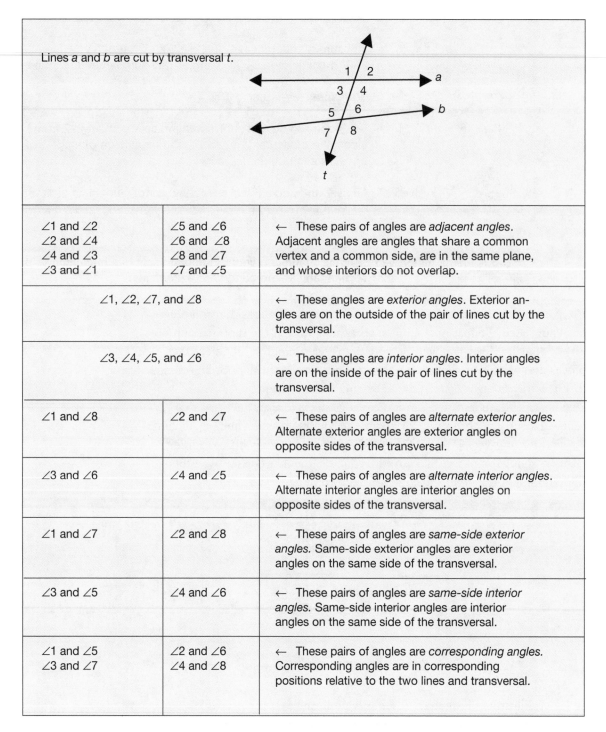

Lines *a* and *b* are cut by transversal *t*.

∠1 and ∠2 ∠2 and ∠4 ∠4 and ∠3 ∠3 and ∠1	∠5 and ∠6 ∠6 and ∠8 ∠8 and ∠7 ∠7 and ∠5	← These pairs of angles are *adjacent angles*. Adjacent angles are angles that share a common vertex and a common side, are in the same plane, and whose interiors do not overlap.
∠1, ∠2, ∠7, and ∠8		← These angles are *exterior angles*. Exterior angles are on the outside of the pair of lines cut by the transversal.
∠3, ∠4, ∠5, and ∠6		← These angles are *interior angles*. Interior angles are on the inside of the pair of lines cut by the transversal.
∠1 and ∠8	∠2 and ∠7	← These pairs of angles are *alternate exterior angles*. Alternate exterior angles are exterior angles on opposite sides of the transversal.
∠3 and ∠6	∠4 and ∠5	← These pairs of angles are *alternate interior angles*. Alternate interior angles are interior angles on opposite sides of the transversal.
∠1 and ∠7	∠2 and ∠8	← These pairs of angles are *same-side exterior angles*. Same-side exterior angles are exterior angles on the same side of the transversal.
∠3 and ∠5	∠4 and ∠6	← These pairs of angles are *same-side interior angles*. Same-side interior angles are interior angles on the same side of the transversal.
∠1 and ∠5 ∠3 and ∠7	∠2 and ∠6 ∠4 and ∠8	← These pairs of angles are *corresponding angles*. Corresponding angles are in corresponding positions relative to the two lines and transversal.

Fig. 3.6. Vocabulary associated with the angles created in a transversal diagram

Once students have a working knowledge of the names of the angles in the transversal diagram, they can begin exploring the angle relationships that are created when a transversal cuts two parallel lines, as shown in the classroom discussion that follows about the following transversal diagram:

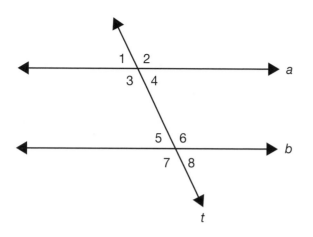

Teacher: On a sheet of notebook paper, sketch this transversal diagram. We are going to assume that lines *a* and *b* are parallel, so you might want to try to make them look that way as much as you can. Then use a protractor to measure all the angles to the nearest degree and label the angles with their measurements.

Teachers should note that in students' diagrams, the measures of angles 1, 4, 5, and 8 should all be approximately equal; the measures of angles 2, 3, 6, and 7 should all be approximately equal; and the sum of the measures of angles 1 and 2 should be approximately 180 degrees. There are various reasons why students might not get angle measures that satisfy these requirements. Teachers might need to help students obtain satisfactory measures by redrawing the lines to be sure they are closer to being parallel or by remeasuring the angles. Students can also do this type of activity on a computer or graphing calculator with geometry exploration software.

Teacher: Who would like to share their measurements?

Bjorn: I would. My measures of angles 1, 4, 5, and 8 in my diagram were all around 60 degrees. Some looked like 58 degrees or 59 degrees; some looked like 62 or 63 degrees. My measures of angles 2, 3, 6, and 7 were all close to 120 degrees.

Teacher: How about the rest of you? [The teacher gives the students time to discuss their results.] So, it seems like, even though we can't make exact measurements, we all seem to agree on about 60 degrees and 120 degrees for the measurements of the two angles. I drew the picture trying to make angle 1 measure 60 degrees, and then the others just ended up as they are because of the measure of angle 1. So, Bjorn, how did you label your diagram?

Bjorn: My diagram looks like this:

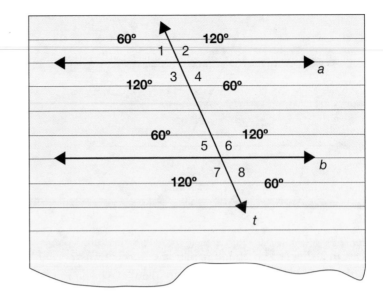

Teacher: What is the sum of the measures of adjacent angles 1 and 2 in Bjorn's diagram? Why does that make sense?

Cat: 60 + 120 = 180, so the sum of the measures of angles 1 and 2 is 180 degrees. That makes sense because angles 1 and 2 form a straight angle and the measure of a straight angle is 180 degrees.

Teacher: That is a good observation, Cat. Let's look at other pairs of angles. What relationships do you see?

At this point, students should look at Bjorn's diagram and notice the following angle relationships that exist when two parallel lines are cut by a transversal:

- alternate interior angles are congruent;

- alternate exterior angles are congruent;

- corresponding angles are congruent;

- same-side interior angles are supplementary;

- same-side exterior angles are supplementary.

Then teachers should have students look at their own diagrams and the diagrams of the others in the class. They should find that in all cases, regardless of the measurements of the angles, these same relationships exist. Through inductive reasoning, then, students can conjecture that these relationships are true for all transversal diagrams that involve parallel lines.

After students have used inductive reasoning to make conjectures about these angle relationships, they can use information about Euclidean geometry to prove that these relationships are true for all transversal diagrams involving parallel lines. With regard to the transversal diagram involving parallel lines, students need to know an accepted truth, or axiom, in Euclidean geometry that is called the corresponding angles axiom: "If two parallel lines are cut by a transversal, then corresponding angles are congruent." This statement is essentially equivalent to the Euclidean parallel postulate that was mentioned before as a distinguishing characteristic between Euclidean and non-Euclidean geometries. On this axiom, or accepted truth, in Euclidean geometry, deductive arguments that prove the other angle relationships can be built.

Classroom discussions, such as the one that follows, can help students begin to understand the deductive reasoning involved in proving the angle relationships in a diagram in which parallel lines are cut by a transversal. Again, teachers would use a diagram like the one shown, where line *a* is parallel to line *b*.

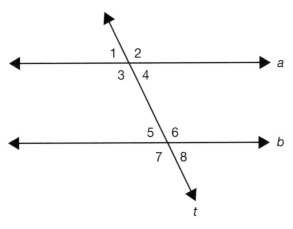

Teacher: We used inductive reasoning to conjecture about the relationships in this transversal diagram. Let's learn how to use deductive reasoning to prove these relationships. If we assume that the axiom "If two parallel lines are cut by a transversal, then corresponding angles are congruent" is true, which angles are congruent?

Marrah: Angles 1 and 5; 2 and 6; 3 and 7; and 4 and 8.

Teacher: Those are the corresponding angles. Now let's choose alternate interior angles. What do we think is true about the relationship between alternate interior angles?

Bob: They are congruent.

Teacher: Okay. Let's now try to prove that alternate interior angles formed by parallel lines cut by a transversal are congruent. We can use any pair of alternate interior angles in the diagram, so let's use angles 3 and 6. A deductive argument is a series of statements connected with logical reasoning. To prove that angle 3 is congruent to angle 6, we need to start with angle relationships that we already know. Let's start with angles 2 and 3. What do you know about angles 2 and 3?

Marrah: They are vertical angles, and we proved that vertical angles are congruent, so angle 2 is congruent to angle 3.

Teacher: Now let's move to angles 2 and 6. What do you know about these angles?

Bob: They are congruent because they are corresponding angles.

Teacher: You have just proved that angle 3 and angle 6 are congruent. Can anyone explain why?

Shakira: I see it! If both angle 3 and angle 6 are congruent to angle 2, then they must be congruent to each other.

Teacher: That makes sense, Shakira. You can write that deductive reasoning more formally like this:

∠2 ≅ ∠3 because they are vertical angles.

∠2 ≅ ∠6 because they are corresponding angles.

If ∠2 ≅ ∠3 and ∠2 ≅ ∠6, then ∠3 ≅ ∠6.

Teacher: We have now proved that if lines *a* and *b* are parallel, then the alternate interior angles formed by the transversal are congruent. So we can now state the following theorem, knowing we have proved it to be true: Alternate interior angles theorem: "If two parallel lines are cut by a transversal, then alternate interior angles are congruent."

Teachers can continue these types of discussions to help students prove the other angle relationship theorems. Note that once a theorem is proved, that theorem can be applied to specific situations and used in a logical argument that proves another theorem. These theorems and deductive arguments that can be used to prove them are shown in figure 3.7.

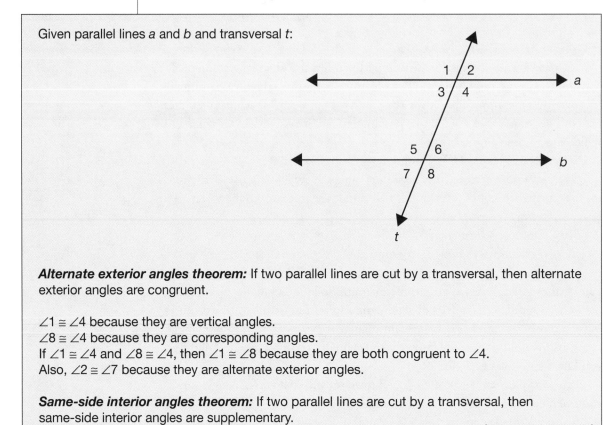

Given parallel lines *a* and *b* and transversal *t*:

Alternate exterior angles theorem: If two parallel lines are cut by a transversal, then alternate exterior angles are congruent.

∠1 ≅ ∠4 because they are vertical angles.
∠8 ≅ ∠4 because they are corresponding angles.
If ∠1 ≅ ∠4 and ∠8 ≅ ∠4, then ∠1 ≅ ∠8 because they are both congruent to ∠4.
Also, ∠2 ≅ ∠7 because they are alternate exterior angles.

Same-side interior angles theorem: If two parallel lines are cut by a transversal, then same-side interior angles are supplementary.

(Continued on next page)

Fig. 3.7. Proving angle relationships when parallel lines are cut by a transversal

$m\angle 3 = m\angle 7$ because corresponding angles are congruent.
$m\angle 5 + m\angle 7 = 180°$ because angles 5 and 7 form a straight angle.
$m\angle 5 + m\angle 3 = 180°$ because angles 3 and 7 are congruent, so you can substitute $m\angle 3$ for $m\angle 7$.

So angles 5 and 3 are supplementary because the sum of their measures is 180°.
Also, angles 5 and 3 are supplementary because they are same-side interior angles.

Same-side exterior angles theorem: If two parallel lines are cut by a transversal, then same-side exterior angles are supplementary.

$m\angle 1 = m\angle 5$ because corresponding angles are congruent.
$m\angle 5 + m\angle 7 = 180°$ because angles 5 and 7 form a straight angle.
$m\angle 1 + m\angle 7 = 180°$ because angles 1 and 5 are congruent, so you can substitute $m\angle 1$ for $m\angle 5$.

So, angles 1 and 7 are supplementary because the sum of their measures is 180°.
Also, angles 2 and 8 are supplementary because they are same-side exterior angles.

Fig. 3.7. Proving angle relationships when parallel lines are cut by a transversal—*Continued*

The sum of the measures of the angles of a triangle

Previously students have worked with triangles and examined the properties of triangles. In grade 8, they learn to use their inductive and deductive reasoning skills to conjecture, and then prove, that the sum of the measures of the angles of a triangle equals 180 degrees. The following classroom discussion illustrates how students can engage in this reasoning.

Teacher: You have explored properties of triangles in earlier grades. Now let's see if we can discover some properties of the angles in a triangle. Draw a triangle on paper. Then rip the paper into three pieces so that there is one vertex of the triangle on each piece. Place the vertices together so that the sides touch. What do you notice?

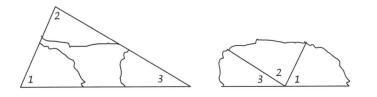

Mia: The angles form a straight angle.
Teacher: That is a good observation, Mia. We know that the measure of a straight angle is 180 degrees, so the sum of the measures of the angles in this triangle seem to be 180 degrees. How can we continue to use inductive reasoning so that we can make a conjecture?

Todd: We do this same activity with many different triangles of all different sizes and see if it seems true for all the triangles we try. If it does, than we can conjecture that the sum of the angles in any triangle is 180 degrees.

Teacher: That is a good idea. One way to do that is to look at every triangle drawn in the class. [The teacher gives students some time to look at one another's examples.] Notice that the triangles were different shapes and sizes, and yet the conjecture appears true for all of them. So let's conjecture that the sum of the angles in any triangle is 180 degrees. But we really don't know if this statement is true or not. Let's see if we can use the definitions and properties we already know are true to create a logical argument that will prove this statement. You already know about some angle relationships that are formed when parallel lines are cut by a transversal. When you are using deductive reasoning to prove a conjecture, always start with what you know. Let's alter our diagram so that the triangle becomes part of a transversal diagram. In this diagram, a and b are parallel and t_1 and t_2 are transversals. The triangle is marked by the angles 1, 2, and 3.

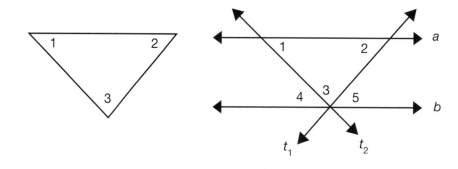

Teacher: Remember that we want to prove that $m\angle 1 + m\angle 2 + m\angle 3 = 180°$. Let's start with angle 3, angle 4 and angle 5. Who can explain what we know about the sum of the measures of angles 4, 3, and 5?

Students: 180 degrees; they form a straight angle.

Teacher: So, we have *something* that has a sum of 180 degrees. But it doesn't involve all of the angles that we want in our sum, just angle 3. How might we get angle 1 involved? Does it have any relationship to angle 4 or 5?

Student: Yes; angle 1 and angle 4 are alternate interior angles, so they are congruent.

Teacher: Yes, we know they are congruent because we made lines a and b parallel. So, we could replace angle 4 in the sum of 180 degrees with angle 1.

Several students at the same time: And we could do the same thing with angles 2 and 5 for the same reasons.

Teacher: So we can substitute angle 1 for angle 4, and angle 2 for angle 5, and say that the sum of the measures of angle 1, angle 3, and angle 2 is 180 degrees.

Todd: I see it. I think it is easier to understand if I write it this way:

- $m\angle 4 + m\angle 3 + m\angle 5 = 180°$ because they make a straight angle.

- $m\angle1 = m\angle4$ because they are alternate interior angles formed by parallel lines and a transversal.

- $m\angle2 = m\angle5$ because they are alternate interior angles formed by parallel lines and a transversal.

- So $m\angle1 + m\angle3 + m\angle2 = 180°$ because you can substitute $m\angle1$ for $m\angle4$ and $m\angle2$ for $m\angle5$.

Teacher: That's logical, Todd. And, it was important for you to include that the alternate interior angles were congruent because they were formed by parallel lines. We have proved that the sum of the measures of the angles of *any* triangle is 180 degrees, and we can now call that statement a theorem: the triangle angle-sum theorem.

After students have proved the triangle angle-sum theorem, they can apply the theorem to find unknown measures of angles, as shown in figure 3.8. In problems such as these, students use their deductive reasoning and apply it to a specific, or particular, situation.

Find the measure of angle C.

$$x + 28 + 34 = 180$$
$$x + 62 = 180$$
$$x + 62 - 62 = 180 - 62$$
$$x = 118$$

The measure of angle C is 118 degrees.

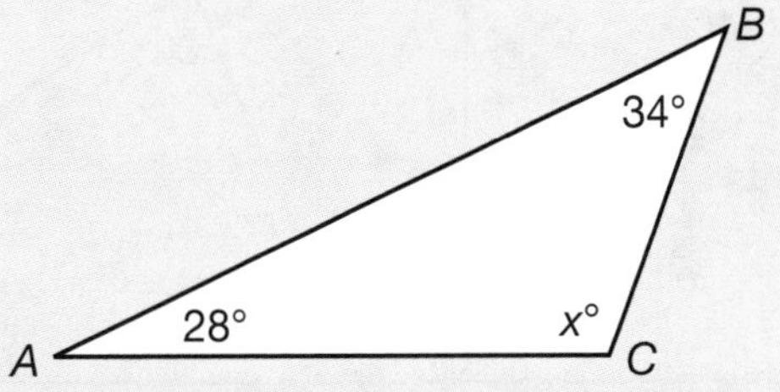

Fig. 3.8. Using the triangle angle-sum theorem to find an unknown angle measure in a triangle

Similar triangles

In grade 7, students learn that similar figures are figures that have the same shape but not necessarily the same size. They learn that two polygons are similar if corresponding angles are congruent and corresponding side lengths are proportional, as illustrated in figure 3.9.

The definition of similar polygons, which applies to triangles, quadrilaterals, pentagons, and all other polygons, includes conditions concerning all sides and all angles of the polygons. But for triangles, not all the conditions need to be known to conclude similarity. One set of information that is sufficient for concluding that two triangles are similar is to know that all three pairs of corresponding angles are congruent. The activity described in figure 3.10 can help students use inductive reasoning to conjecture that if the corresponding angles in two triangles are congruent, the triangles are similar.

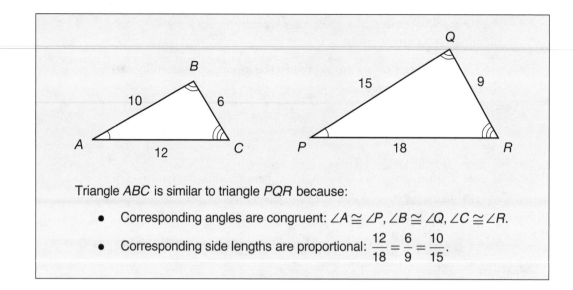

Triangle *ABC* is similar to triangle *PQR* because:

- Corresponding angles are congruent: $\angle A \cong \angle P$, $\angle B \cong \angle Q$, $\angle C \cong \angle R$.
- Corresponding side lengths are proportional: $\frac{12}{18} = \frac{6}{9} = \frac{10}{15}$.

Fig. 3.9. Triangles that satisfy the definition of similar polygons

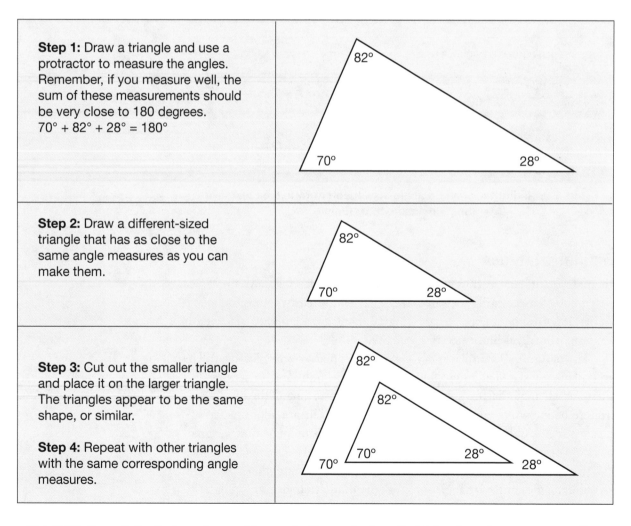

Step 1: Draw a triangle and use a protractor to measure the angles. Remember, if you measure well, the sum of these measurements should be very close to 180 degrees.
$70° + 82° + 28° = 180°$

Step 2: Draw a different-sized triangle that has as close to the same angle measures as you can make them.

Step 3: Cut out the smaller triangle and place it on the larger triangle. The triangles appear to be the same shape, or similar.

Step 4: Repeat with other triangles with the same corresponding angle measures.

Fig. 3.10. An activity that can be used to create the conjecture that triangles whose corresponding angles are congruent are similar

As students complete the activity, teachers should encourage them to look for other properties and patterns. For example, students might realize during step 2 that when they make two angles of the second triangle congruent to two angles of the first triangle, then the third angle of the second triangle will be automatically congruent to its corresponding angle in the first triangle because the sum of the measures of the angles in every triangle is 180 degrees. These types of insights will deepen students' understanding of the relationships they are exploring. After students have completed the activity once, they can also explore the result that the corresponding sides of the pairs of triangles they created are proportional. Then teachers should have students complete the activity several more times and have students consolidate their results before making a conjecture about the angles. Once students have used their observations to make a conjecture, teachers can affirm that it is possible with additional geometric ideas to deductively prove what students have used inductive reasoning to conjecture—triangles are similar if their corresponding angles are congruent.

Students can then use this theorem in conjunction with what they know about angles and parallel lines to deductively prove other conjectures concerning similar triangles. For example, as illustrated in the following class discussion, students can prove that if a line is drawn through two sides of a triangle, parallel to the third side of the triangle, the new triangle formed is similar to the original triangle.

Teacher: In geometry, mathematicians use axioms and theorems that they have proved to deductively prove other conjectures. We have learned a lot about angles in similar triangles and about angle relationships in transversal diagrams that involve parallel lines. Let's use these axioms and theorems to prove another theorem. Start with triangle *ABC*.

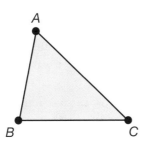

Now draw the line that contains side *BC* of the triangle. Then draw a line parallel to line *BC*, intersecting the other two sides of the triangle. Name the points of intersection *E* and *D*, with *E* on side *AB*.

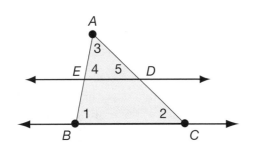

Teacher: Compare the new triangle *AED* and triangle *ABC*. What do you notice?

Marrah: It looks to me that triangle *AED* is similar to triangle *ABC*.

Teacher: Interesting observation. If they were similar, what would be true about their angles?

Marrah: Corresponding angles would be congruent.

Teacher: Actually, Marrah, if we were to draw this figure with different-sized triangles, we would see the same result. The smaller triangle looks similar to the original triangle. Can you tell me how we could prove that the triangles are similar?

Bob: I think that we can use that theorem we talked about. If you can show that corresponding angles are congruent, then you know that the triangles are similar.

Teacher: Bob's statement is correct. If we can show that the new triangle created, triangle *AED,* has angles that are congruent to the corresponding angles in original triangle *ABC,* then we will have proved that the triangles are similar. What are the angles in triangle *ABC?* [1, 2, and 3] What are the angles of triangle *AED?* [3, 4, and 5] What angles do you need to prove are congruent?

Bjorn: I need to prove that angle 1 is congruent to angle 4 and that angle 2 is congruent to angle 5 because those are corresponding angles. Angle 3 is in both triangles, so its measure doesn't change.

Teacher: That's a good observation. That is actually the reflexive property of congruence: an angle is congruent to itself. Think about the angle relationships you found in parallel lines cut by a transversal. Does anyone see how to prove that these angles are congruent?

Bob: I do! Look, the diagram is actually a transversal diagram where line *ED* is parallel to line *BC* and side *AB* is a transversal. If you look at it that way, angle 1 and angle 4 are corresponding angles, so we know that they are congruent.

Marrah: I see it, too. Side *AC* is also a transversal that cuts the two parallel lines. Angle 2 is congruent to angle 5 for the same reason; they are corresponding angles.

Teacher: Those deductive arguments are logical. And we know that angle 3 is congruent to itself. Who can summarize our reasoning?

Todd: I think I can:

- $\angle 1 \cong \angle 4$ because they are corresponding angles formed by parallel lines and a transversal;

- $\angle 2 \cong \angle 5$ because they are corresponding angles formed by parallel lines and a transversal;

- $\angle 3 \cong \angle 3$ because any angle is congruent to itself.

So $\triangle ABC$ is similar to $\triangle AED$ because all corresponding angles are congruent.

Students should understand that once they have proved the relationship for a line parallel to one side of the triangle, because the same argument would apply no matter which side of the triangle they chose, they can know it is true for all sides of the triangle, as shown in figure 3.11.

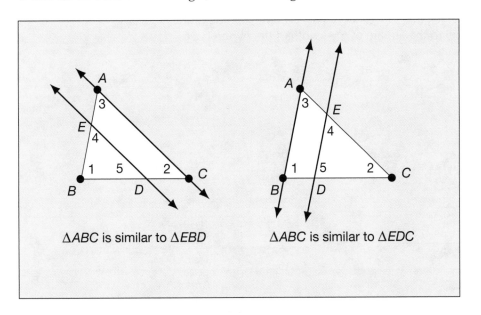

Fig. 3.11. Examples showing that a line drawn parallel to any side of a triangle creates similar triangles

At this grade, students should consider all angles in a triangle to show similarity. However, as students' experience with situations involving similar triangles increases, they may begin to realize that only two pairs of congruent angles are needed to ensure similarity. In later grades students will encounter the angle-angle (AA) similarity theorem. The theorem states formally what students may begin to understand intuitively—that if two angles of one triangle are congruent to two angles of another triangle, then the triangles are similar.

The Pythagorean theorem and its converse

As students continue to investigate geometric figures and space by using angle and distance, they can begin to develop an appreciation for the special relationship that exists among the lengths of the sides of a right triangle. This relationship is represented by the Pythagorean theorem, that is, that if a and b are the lengths of the legs of a right triangle and c is the length of the hypotenuse, $a^2 + b^2 = c^2$, as shown in figure 3.12.

Students' initial experiences with right triangles and the Pythagorean theorem should be concrete. For example, students can see the relationship among the lengths of the sides of the right triangle through activities such as the one illustrated in figure 3.13.

Students can repeat this activity using other squares with whole-number lengths, for example 6, 8, and 10; and 5, 12, and 13. Although this activity is most meaningful if completed with whole-number side lengths, it allows students to use their previous knowledge about triangles, squares, and area to

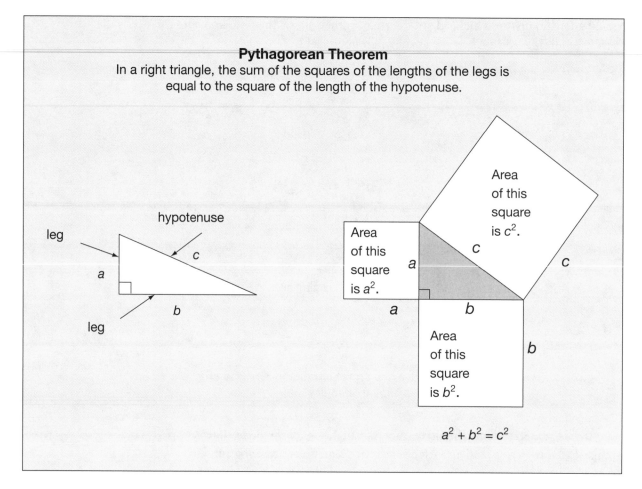

Pythagorean Theorem
In a right triangle, the sum of the squares of the lengths of the legs is equal to the square of the length of the hypotenuse.

$$a^2 + b^2 = c^2$$

Fig. 3.12. A geometric representation of the Pythagorean theorem

understand the new concept of the Pythagorean theorem. Through it, students can conjecture that when the lengths of the sides of the squares form a right triangle, the sum of the areas of the smaller cut-out squares is equal to the area of the larger square.

It is beneficial for students to explore the relationships presented in the Pythagorean theorem in a variety of ways. Although the activity shown in figure 3.13 is illustrative when the lengths of the sides are whole numbers, other activities result in representations that can be constructed using right triangles with any side lengths, including fractional side lengths. In these activities, the emphasis is on the relationships among the side lengths, not the measurements themselves; in fact, the side lengths remain unknown.

Reflect As You Read

Why is it important for students to be able to think about geometric relationships without specific numerical values attached? How can this ability relate to preparation for algebra?

Activity

Step 1: On grid paper, draw a right triangle with legs 3 units and 4 units. Measure the hypotenuse to confirm that it is 5 units long.

Step 2: Draw squares such that a side of each square is a side of the triangle and the interiors of the squares are in the exterior of the triangle.

Step 3: Find the area of each square. Label the area of the squares, that is, $a^2 = 9$, $b^2 = 16$, $c^2 = 25$.

Step 4: Make a conjecture about the relationship between c^2 and the sum of a^2 and b^2.

In this right triangle

$a^2 = 3^2 = 9$
$b^2 = 4^2 = 16$
$c^2 = 5^2 = 25$; and
$3^2 + 4^2 = 5^2$
$9 + 16 = 25$
$25 = 25$

So it looks like for this right triangle, $a^2 + b^2 = c^2$.

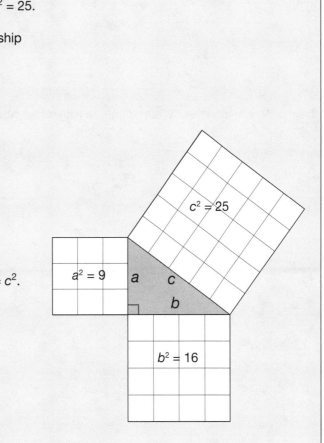

Fig. 3.13. Activity illustrating the Pythagorean theorem

Activities such as the one shown in figure 3.14 allow students to connect a visual, geometric representation of the Pythagorean theorem with an algebraic representation.

Activity:

Step 1: Cut out four copies of the same right triangle. Identify the leg lengths as *a* and *b* and the hypotenuse length as *c*.

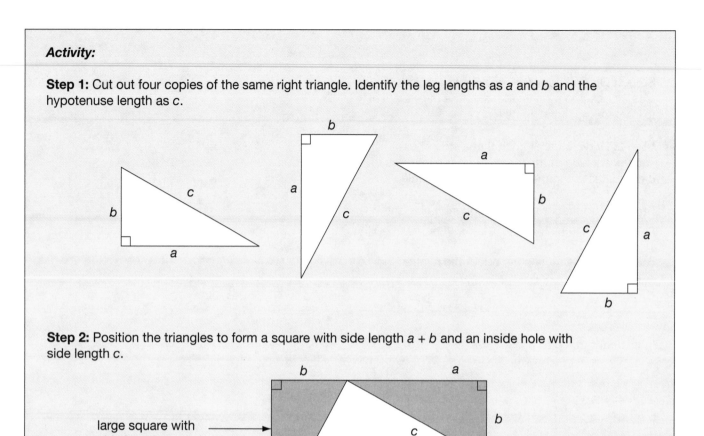

Step 2: Position the triangles to form a square with side length *a* + *b* and an inside hole with side length *c*.

large square with
side length *a* + *b*

square hole with
side length *c*

Step 3: Reason as follows:
- Each of the four triangles has an area of $\frac{ab}{2}$.

- The hole is a square, since the angles have to be right angles because the other two angles are the acute angles in a right triangle and add to 90 degrees. The area of the square hole is c^2.

- The area of the large square with side length *a* + *b* is $(a + b)^2$, and its area is the sum of the areas of the hole and the four triangles.

So $(a + b)^2 = c^2 + 4 \cdot \dfrac{ab}{2}$.

(Continued on next page)

Fig. 3.14. Linking a geometric representation with an algebraic representation to validate the Pythagorean theorem

Step 4: Use the distributive property to simplify the equation, and then use properties of equality to rewrite it in terms of c^2.

$$(a+b)^2 = c^2 + 4 \cdot \frac{ab}{2}$$

$$a^2 + 2ab + b^2 = c^2 + 4 \cdot \frac{ab}{2}$$

$$a^2 + 2ab + b^2 = c^2 + 2ab$$

$$a^2 + 2ab - 2ab + b^2 = c^2 + 2ab - 2ab$$

$$a^2 + b^2 = c^2$$

So $c^2 = b^2 + a^2$ for each of the four cut-out right triangles.

Fig. 3.14. Linking a geometric representation with an algebraic representation to validate the Pythagorean theorem—*Continued*

Once students have demonstrated the validity of the Pythagorean theorem and understand the relationship among the sides of a right triangle, students can apply the Pythagorean theorem to find a missing side length of a right triangle when given the other two side lengths, as shown in figure 3.15.

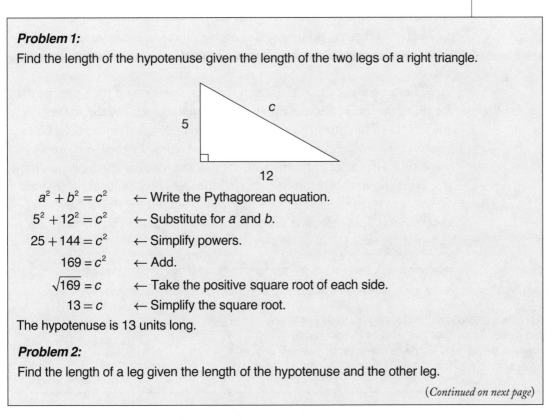

Problem 1:

Find the length of the hypotenuse given the length of the two legs of a right triangle.

$a^2 + b^2 = c^2$ ← Write the Pythagorean equation.

$5^2 + 12^2 = c^2$ ← Substitute for a and b.

$25 + 144 = c^2$ ← Simplify powers.

$169 = c^2$ ← Add.

$\sqrt{169} = c$ ← Take the positive square root of each side.

$13 = c$ ← Simplify the square root.

The hypotenuse is 13 units long.

Problem 2:

Find the length of a leg given the length of the hypotenuse and the other leg.

(*Continued on next page*)

Fig. 3.15. Applying the Pythagorean theorem

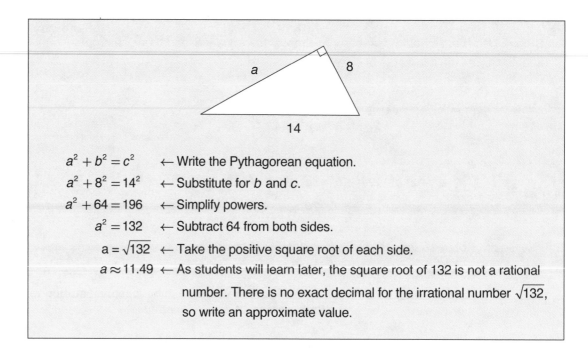

$a^2 + b^2 = c^2$ ← Write the Pythagorean equation.

$a^2 + 8^2 = 14^2$ ← Substitute for b and c.

$a^2 + 64 = 196$ ← Simplify powers.

$a^2 = 132$ ← Subtract 64 from both sides.

$a = \sqrt{132}$ ← Take the positive square root of each side.

$a \approx 11.49$ ← As students will learn later, the square root of 132 is not a rational number. There is no exact decimal for the irrational number $\sqrt{132}$, so write an approximate value.

Fig. 3.15. Applying the Pythagorean theorem—*Continued*

In grade 8, students will encounter square roots in meaningful contexts, such as when applying the Pythagorean theorem. They will begin to extend their understanding of number as they learn about rational and irrational numbers and that the positive square roots of some numbers are irrational. More about irrational numbers is found in the Connections section later in this chapter.

The converse of the Pythagorean theorem states that if the square of the length of the longest side of a triangle is equal to the sum of the squares of the lengths of the other two sides, then the triangle is a right triangle. Once students understand that the relationship represented by the Pythagorean equation exists for all right triangles, they are ready to use the converse of the Pythagorean theorem to prove that a triangle is or is not a right triangle. Students can revisit activities such as the one found in figure 3.13 and use them as an inductive look at the converse of the Pythagorean theorem, as shown in figure 3.16.

Activity

Step 1: Cut out squares with side lengths 3, 4, and 5 from grid paper. Note that the sum of the areas of the two smaller squares is equal to the area of the largest square.

(*Continued on next page*)

Fig. 3.16. Activity illustrating the converse of the Pythagorean theorem

Step 2: Position the squares as shown to form a triangle with side lengths 3, 4, and 5. Note that there is only one triangle that can be created with these three lengths.

Step 3: Make a conjecture about what kind of triangle these lengths seem to form.

We know that—

$$a^2 + b^2 = c^2$$
$$3^2 + 4^2 = 5^2$$
$$9 + 16 = 25$$
$$25 = 25$$

And it looks like the triangle formed is a right triangle.

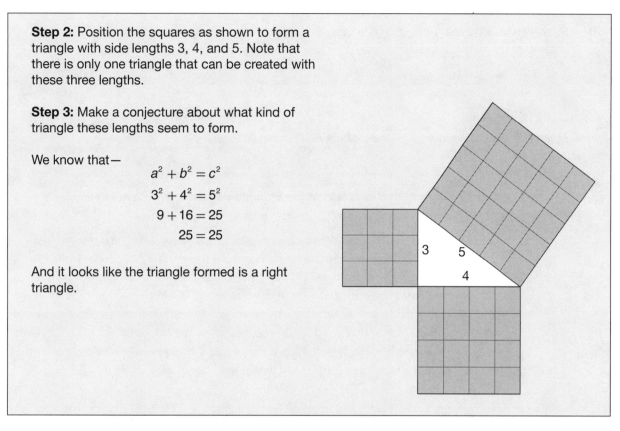

Fig. 3.16. Activity illustrating the converse of the Pythagorean theorem—*Continued*

Although this activity is most meaningful only if completed with whole-number side lengths, it allows students to use their previous knowledge to understand the new concept of the converse of the Pythagorean theorem. Through it, students can observe and verify that when the sum of the areas of the smaller cut-out squares is equal to the area of the larger square, the lengths of the sides of the squares form a right triangle.

Once students understand the converse of the Pythagorean theorem, they can use it to solve problems. Examples of how students can use the converse of the Pythagorean theorem are shown in figure 3.17.

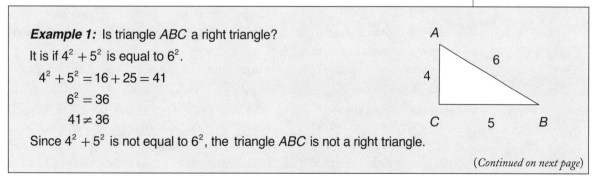

Example 1: Is triangle *ABC* a right triangle?

It is if $4^2 + 5^2$ is equal to 6^2.

$$4^2 + 5^2 = 16 + 25 = 41$$
$$6^2 = 36$$
$$41 \neq 36$$

Since $4^2 + 5^2$ is not equal to 6^2, the triangle *ABC* is not a right triangle.

(*Continued on next page*)

Fig. 3.17. Applying the converse of the Pythagorean theorem

Example 2: Is triangle *PQR* a right triangle?

It is if $2.5^2 + 6^2$ is equal to 6.5^2.

$2.5^2 + 6^2 = 6.25 + 36 = 42.25$

$6.5^2 = 42.25$

$42.25 = 42.25$

Since $2.5^2 + 6^2$ is equal to 6.5^2, the triangle *PQR* is a right triangle.

Fig. 3.17. Applying the converse of the Pythagorean theorem—*Continued*

As students explore the Pythagorean theorem and its converse, it is beneficial for them to learn about Pythagorean triples. A Pythagorean triple is a set of three whole numbers that can be lengths of sides of a right triangle. Students can verify that a set of three numbers is a Pythagorean triple by using the equation $a^2 + b^2 = c^2$. If the numbers satisfy this equation, the numbers form a Pythagorean triple and can be the lengths of the sides of a right triangle with *c* the length of the hypotenuse. Examples of Pythagorean triples and triples that are not Pythagorean triples are shown with verification in figure 3.18.

$a = 3, b = 4, c = 5$	$a = 8, b = 11, c = 13$	$a = 5, b = 12, c = 13$
Does $a^2 + b^2 = c^2$?	Does $a^2 + b^2 = c^2$?	Does $a^2 + b^2 = c^2$?
$3^2 + 4^2 = 9 + 16 = 25$	$8^2 + 11^2 = 64 + 121 = 185$	$5^2 + 12^2 = 25 + 144 = 169$
$5^2 = 25$	$13^2 = 169$	$13^2 = 169$
So 3, 4, 5 is a Pythagorean triple.	So 8, 11, 13 is not a Pythagorean triple.	So 5, 12, 13 is a Pythagorean triple.

Fig. 3.18. Verifying Pythagorean triples

Students learn that if they know a Pythagorean triple, they can generate more Pythagorean triples by using multiples of the numbers in the known triple, as shown in figure 3.19.

Students should realize that the columns in figure 3.19 continue without end. Students can verify that the triangles with these sides are also right triangles by using the converse of the Pythagorean theorem, as shown in figure 3.17. Students will benefit by learning some of the common Pythagorean triples; they will find it useful to know some of them as they explore right-triangle relationships in grade 8 and in later grades. Several of the most common Pythagorean triples are the following:

3, 4, 5   5, 12, 13   7, 24, 25   8, 15, 17   9, 40, 41   11, 60, 61

	Multiples of 3, 4, 5	Multiples of 5, 12, 13	Multiples of 8, 15, 17
Multiply by 1:	3, 4, 5	5, 12, 13	8, 15, 17
Multiply by 2:	6, 8, 10	10, 24, 26	16, 30, 34
Multiply by 3:	9, 12, 15	15, 36, 39	24, 45, 51
Multiply by 4:	12, 16, 20	20, 48, 52	32, 60, 68

Fig. 3.19. Generating Pythagorean triples

Focusing on analyzing geometric figures and space through problem solving

In grade 8, problem-solving experiences should include rich problems that require students to bring together different concepts, such as measurement, similarity, ratio and proportion, area and volume, angle relationships, and the Pythagorean theorem. Computation with rational numbers should also be included. Problems such as the ones shown in figure 3.20 allow students to apply a variety of their developing skills.

Problem 1: Tree Shadow Problem
At a certain time of day, a person 5 feet tall casts a shadow 8 feet long. At the same time, a tree casts a shadow 20 feet long. What is the height of the tree?

Solution:
The triangles formed are similar because their corresponding angles are congruent. So the ratios of their corresponding parts are equal.

$$\frac{5}{8} = \frac{h}{20}$$
$$8h = 5 \times 20$$
$$8h = 100$$
$$\frac{8h}{8} = \frac{100}{8}$$
$$h = 12\frac{1}{2}$$

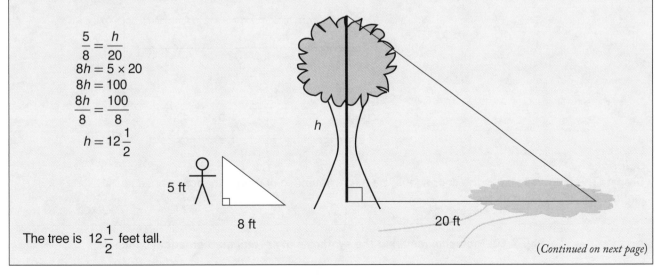

The tree is $12\frac{1}{2}$ feet tall.

(Continued on next page)

Fig. 3.20. Problems requiring the synthesis of several mathematical concepts

Required ideas: Synthesis of geometric models, measurement concepts, similarity, ratio and proportion, and computation with rational numbers

Problem 2: Ridge Highway Problem

A plot of land in the shape of a right triangle is bounded on two sides by Ridge Highway and Route 16, as shown in the diagram. The third boundary is the line segment *AB*. Find the perimeter and area of the plot of land.

Solution:

Let *x* represent the distance *AB*.

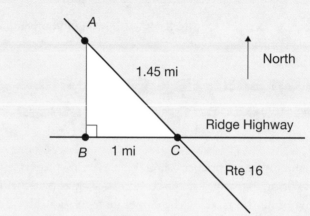

$$1^2 + x^2 = 1.45^2$$
$$1 + x^2 = 2.1025$$
$$x^2 = 1.1025$$
$$x = \sqrt{1.1025}$$
$$x = 1.05$$

Perimeter = 1.05 + 1 + 1.45 = 3.5

Area = $\dfrac{1}{2}(1)(1.05) = 0.525$

The perimeter is 3.5 miles, and the area is 0.525 square mile.

Required ideas: Synthesis of geometric models, measurement concepts, the Pythagorean theorem, perimeter, area, and computation with rational numbers

Problem 3: Office Construction Problem

The diagram represents an office space under construction. The office is supposed to be in the shape of a rectangular prism 32 feet long, 24 feet wide, and 9 feet high. A foreman is measuring distances to check that all angles formed by the edges are right angles. What should be the diagonal distance d_1 across the floor and the space diagonal distance d_2 from floor to ceiling if all angles formed by the edges are right angles?

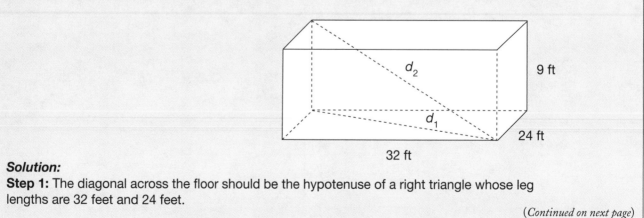

Solution:

Step 1: The diagonal across the floor should be the hypotenuse of a right triangle whose leg lengths are 32 feet and 24 feet.

(Continued on next page)

Fig. 3.20. Problems requiring the synthesis of several mathematical concepts

$$32^2 + 24^2 = \left(d_1\right)^2$$
$$1024 + 576 = \left(d_1\right)^2$$
$$1600 = \left(d_1\right)^2$$
$$\sqrt{1600} = d_1$$
$$40 = d_1$$

Step 2: The diagonal from the opposite corner of the floor to ceiling (a space diagonal of the prism) should be the hypotenuse of a right triangle whose leg lengths are 40 feet and 9 feet.

$$40^2 + 9^2 = \left(d_2\right)^2$$
$$1600 + 81 = \left(d_2\right)^2$$
$$1681 = \left(d_2\right)^2$$
$$\sqrt{1681} = d_2$$
$$41 = d_2$$

The diagonal distance d_1 across the floor should be 40 feet, and the space diagonal distance d_2 from floor to ceiling should be 41 feet.

Required ideas: Synthesis of three-dimensional geometric models, measurement concepts, the Pythagorean theorem, properties of a polyhedron, and computation with rational numbers

Problem 4: Landscape Problem

A landscape architect is working on a design for triangular lot *PQR* that has side lengths 50 meters, 40 meters, and 32.2 meters. He is planning a straight path from point *A* to point *B*, parallel to the 40-meter side. Point *B* is 12 meters from point *R*. He needs to know the angle measures labeled *x* degrees and *y* degrees and the length of the path *AB*. What are the values of *x* and *y*? What is the length of the path *AB*? Explain your reasoning.

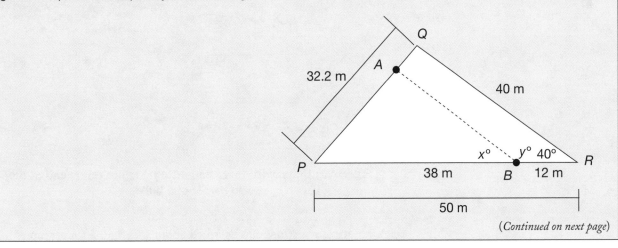

(*Continued on next page*)

Fig. 3.20. Problems requiring the synthesis of several mathematical concepts

Solution:
The angle labeled *x* degrees and the 40-degree angle are corresponding angles formed by parallel lines and a transversal, so they are congruent. The angle labeled *y* degrees and the 40 degree angle are same-side interior angles formed by parallel lines and a transversal, so they are supplementary; so *x* = 40, *y* = 140.

Triangles *PQR* and *PAB* are similar because $\overline{AB}$ is parallel to $\overline{QR}$, so the sides are proportional.

The length of path *AB* is 30.4 meters.

$$\frac{AB}{40} = \frac{38}{50}$$
$$50\,AB = 40 \cdot 38$$
$$50\,AB = 1520$$
$$\frac{50\,AB}{50} = \frac{1520}{50}$$
$$AB = 30.4$$

Required ideas: Synthesis of geometric models, measurement concepts, similarity, ratio and proportion, angle relationships, and computation with rational numbers

Fig. 3.20. Problems requiring the synthesis of several mathematical concepts—*Continued*

Teachers can alter problems such as the ones in figure 3.20 to include a variety of rational numbers, including decimal and fractional values. It is beneficial for students to use technology as they learn to solve such problems, so that the focus remains on how to solve the problems rather than on the more complicated computation.

Teachers should also present students with opportunities to explore a variety of mathematical relationships that exist in more complex figures such as the one in figure 3.21. This figure is a diagram of a composite three-dimensional figure consisting of a rectangular prism topped by a triangular prism. The triangle in the diagram is isosceles. The figure represents a scale model of a building with a scale of 1 inch : 20 inches.

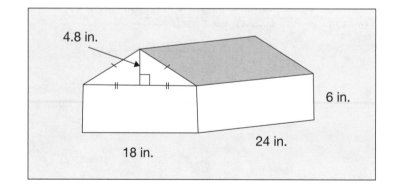

Fig. 3.21. Composite three-dimensional figure representing the scale model of a building

A variety of questions can be asked about this figure, for example:

a. What are the actual dimensions of the building in feet?

b. The four walls and two triangular surfaces will be painted on the exterior. What is the area that will be painted?

c. The roof, consisting of two congruent rectangles, one of which is shown (shaded), will be covered with shingles. What is the actual roof area that will be shingled?

d. What is the total volume of the building?

To solve problems such as these, students need to apply their understandings of measurement, similarity, ratio and proportion, area and volume, the Pythagorean theorem, computation with rational numbers, and characteristics of polyhedra. Solutions to some of these problems are shown in figure 3.22.

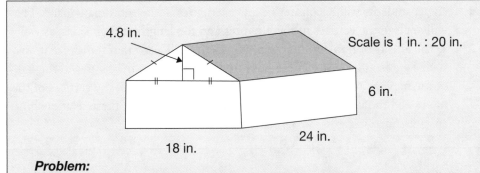

Problem:
What are the actual dimensions of the building in feet?

Solution:
$20 \times 4.8 = 96$ and $96 \div 12 = 8$, so the triangular surface is 8 feet high.
$20 \times 18 = 360$ and $360 \div 12 = 30$, so the building is 30 feet wide.
$20 \times 24 = 480$ and $480 \div 12 = 40$, so the building is 40 feet long.
$20 \times 6 = 120$ and $120 \div 12 = 10$, so the walls are 10 feet high.

Problem:
The roof, consisting of two congruent rectangles, one of which is shown (shaded), will be covered with shingles. What is the actual roof area that will be shingled?

Solution:
To find the area of a rectangular roof surface, first find the length of the hypotenuse of the right triangle whose leg lengths are 8 feet and 15 feet.

$$8^2 + 15^2 = x^2$$
$$64 + 225 = x^2$$
$$289 = x^2$$
$$\sqrt{289} = x$$
$$17 = x$$

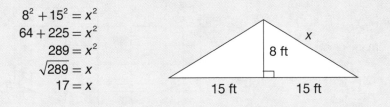

Each rectangular roof surface is a rectangle 17 feet by 40 feet.
Area of two rectangular roof surfaces: $2 \times 17 \times 40 = 1{,}360$
The roof area to be shingled is 1,360 square feet.

Fig. 3.22. Solutions to problems associated with a complex three-dimensional figure

Focusing on Figures and Space through Connections

As students analyze two- and three-dimensional space and figures by using distance and angle, their understanding can deepen when they make connections to other mathematical concepts. Teachers should point out connections to such concepts as coordinate geometry, trigonometric ratios, special right triangles, square roots and irrational numbers, and angle relationships in polygons.

In the study of analyzing two-dimensional figures by using distance and angle, students will encounter geometric figures in the coordinate plane. They will analyze the vertices of these figures and the length of their sides, as well as the effects of transforming them. Students will learn that transformations such as reflections, translations, and rotations of geometric figures in the co-ordinate plane result in patterns and relationships between the vertices of the figure and the vertices of the transformed figure. Some of these relationships are illustrated in figure 3.23.

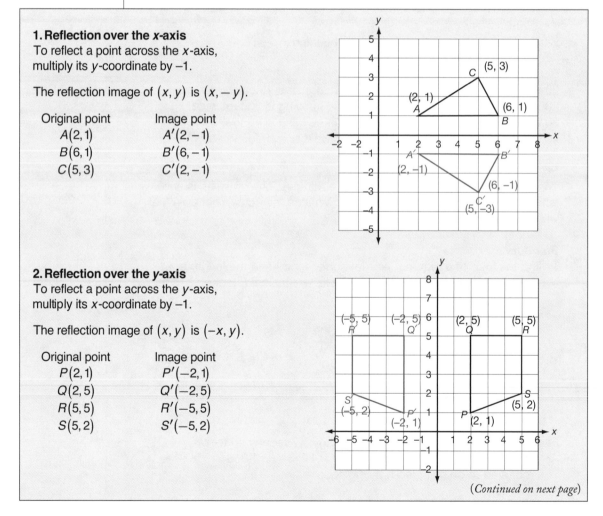

1. Reflection over the *x*-axis
To reflect a point across the *x*-axis, multiply its *y*-coordinate by –1.

The reflection image of (x, y) is $(x, -y)$.

Original point	Image point
$A(2,1)$	$A'(2,-1)$
$B(6,1)$	$B'(6,-1)$
$C(5,3)$	$C'(2,-1)$

2. Reflection over the *y*-axis
To reflect a point across the *y*-axis, multiply its *x*-coordinate by –1.

The reflection image of (x, y) is $(-x, y)$.

Original point	Image point
$P(2,1)$	$P'(-2,1)$
$Q(2,5)$	$Q'(-2,5)$
$R(5,5)$	$R'(-5,5)$
$S(5,2)$	$S'(-5,2)$

(*Continued on next page*)

Fig. 3.23. Examples showing the relationships between original points and images of certain transformations in the coordinate plane

3. Translation

The image of (x, y) after a translation 4 units left and 2 units up is $(x - 4, y + 2)$.

Original point	Image point
$D(3, -3)$	$D'(-1, -1)$
$E(3, 2)$	$E'(-1, 4)$
$F(5, 2)$	$F'(1, 4)$

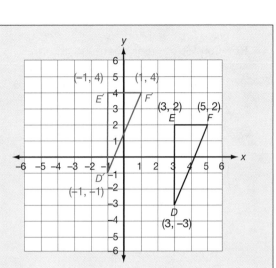

4. Rotation 90 degrees clockwise about the origin

To rotate a point 90 degrees clockwise about the origin, interchange the coordinates and then multiply the new second coordinate by –1.

The rotation image of (x, y) is $(y, -x)$

Original point	Image point
$P(2, 1)$	$P'(1, -2)$
$Q(2, 5)$	$Q'(5, -2)$
$R(5, 5)$	$R'(5, -5)$
$S(5, 2)$	$S'(2, -5)$

5. Rotation 90 degrees counterclockwise about the origin

To rotate a point 90 degrees counterclockwise about the origin, interchange the coordinates and then multiply the new first coordinate by –1.

The rotation image of (x, y) is $(-y, x)$

Original point	Image point
$T(1, 2)$	$T'(-2, 1)$
$U(5, 4)$	$U'(-4, 5)$

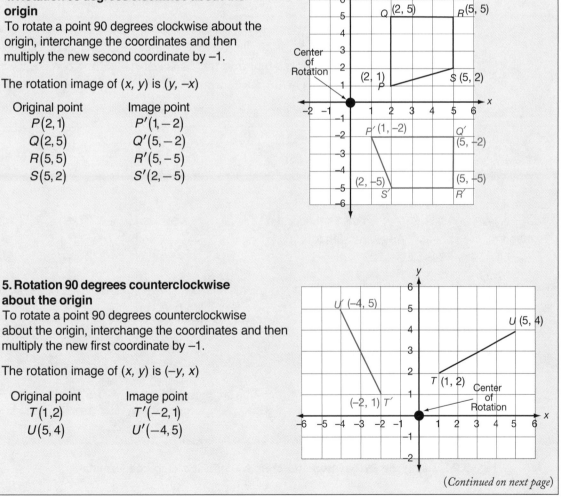

(*Continued on next page*)

Fig. 3.23. Examples showing the relationships between original points and images of certain transformations in the coordinate plane

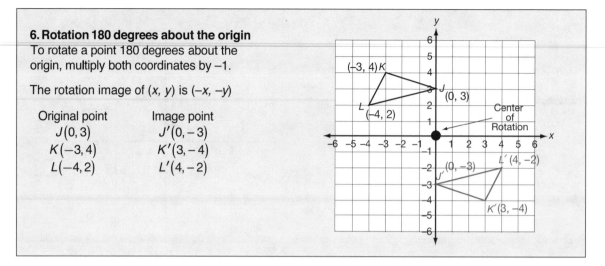

6. Rotation 180 degrees about the origin

To rotate a point 180 degrees about the origin, multiply both coordinates by –1.

The rotation image of (x, y) is $(-x, -y)$

Original point	Image point
$J(0, 3)$	$J'(0, -3)$
$K(-3, 4)$	$K'(3, -4)$
$L(-4, 2)$	$L'(4, -2)$

Fig. 3.23. Examples showing the relationships between original points and images of certain transformations in the coordinate plane—*Continued*

In students' work with analyzing plane figures by using length and angle, they can make a connection to the distance formula. Students learn that the distance formula allows them to find the distance between any two points on the coordinate plane. The distance formula is based on the Pythagorean theorem, as shown in figure 3.24.

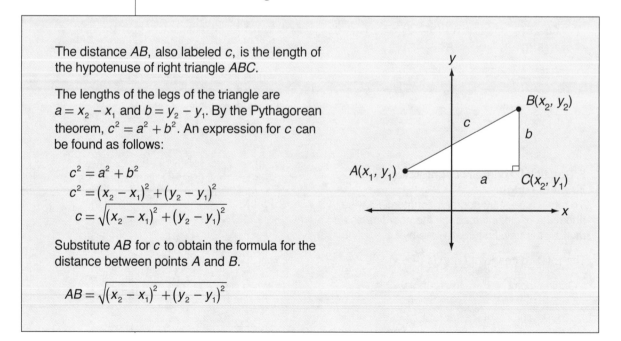

The distance AB, also labeled c, is the length of the hypotenuse of right triangle ABC.

The lengths of the legs of the triangle are $a = x_2 - x_1$ and $b = y_2 - y_1$. By the Pythagorean theorem, $c^2 = a^2 + b^2$. An expression for c can be found as follows:

$$c^2 = a^2 + b^2$$
$$c^2 = (x_2 - x_1)^2 + (y_2 - y_1)^2$$
$$c = \sqrt{(x_2 - x_1)^2 + (y_2 - y_1)^2}$$

Substitute AB for c to obtain the formula for the distance between points A and B.

$$AB = \sqrt{(x_2 - x_1)^2 + (y_2 - y_1)^2}$$

Fig. 3.24. Using the Pythagorean theorem to write the distance formula

Students can learn to apply the distance formula as shown in figure 3.25.

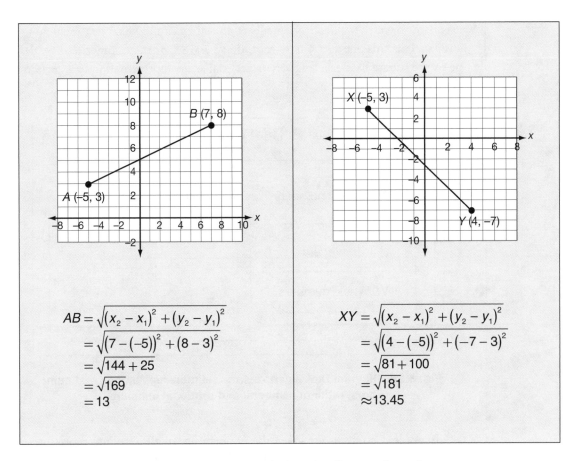

Fig. 3.25. Examples using the distance formula

During their work with the Pythagorean theorem and the distance formula, students begin to encounter square roots and irrational numbers. In grade 7, students encountered irrational numbers in a limited way, for example, when they used π in their work with circles. In grade 8, students expand on this basic understanding as they learn that irrational numbers are numbers that cannot be represented in the form *a/b*, where *a* and *b* are integers and *b* ≠ 0; therefore an irrational number does not have a repeating or terminating decimal representation. Students learn that some irrational numbers are represented by special symbols such as π or $\sqrt{2}$ (read *the square root of two*). They expand their understanding of number as they learn how irrational numbers are related to the numbers in other number systems about which they have previously learned, and about their relationship to the set of the real numbers, as illustrated in figure 3.26.

As students encounter square roots in their work with the Pythagorean theorem and the distance formula, they learn that the positive square roots of some numbers are irrational numbers. For example, in figure 3.25, the distance between *X* and *Y* is $\sqrt{181}$. When they calculate the square root of 181, for example by using a calculator or a square root table, they should be made aware that $\sqrt{181}$ is an irrational number; that is, it cannot be expressed as a terminating or repeating decimal, even though it may appear that way on the calculator or in the table. Students learn that they can leave an irrational answer such as this one as a square root, that is, $\sqrt{181}$, or they can write the value of the square root as a fraction or decimal as an approximation to a certain degree of accuracy, that is, $\sqrt{181} \approx 13.45$.

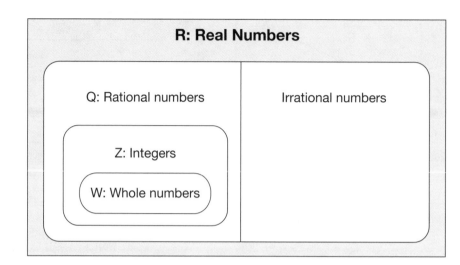

Fig. 3.26. Diagram that illustrates the relationships among real numbers, rational numbers, and irrational numbers

In grade 8, students are given the opportunity to glimpse into more sophisticated mathematics topics such as trigonometry. Students learn that trigonometry is based largely on right triangles. Every right triangle has two acute angles, and associated with each acute angle are six ratios that are made up of the lengths of sides of the triangle. These trigonometric ratios are called sine, cosine, tangent, cotangent, secant, and cosecant. The first three—sine, cosine, and tangent (abbreviated sin, cos, and tan)—are the most commonly used. The definitions of the sine, cosine, and tangent ratios are given in figure 3.27, using angle *A* of the right triangle.

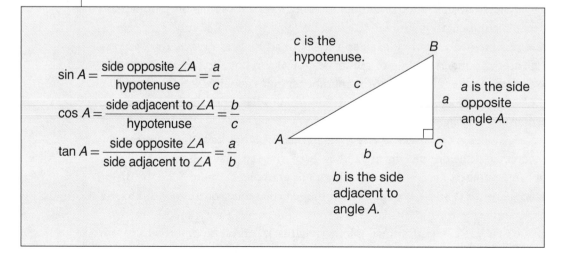

Fig. 3.27. Definitions of three trigonometric ratios

Figure 3.28 shows the sine, cosine, and tangent ratios for the acute angles in a 3-4-5 right triangle.

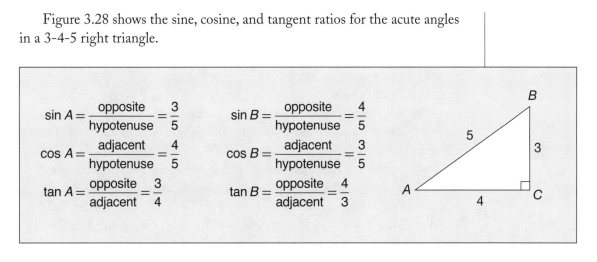

Fig. 3.28. Trigonometric ratios for the acute angles in a 3-4-5 triangle

Similarity plays a key role in trigonometric ratios. Recall that an angle is the union of two rays. Figure 3.29 shows angle A as the union of the two rays $\overrightarrow{AP}$ and $\overrightarrow{AQ}$. Also shown are line segments from $\overrightarrow{AP}$ perpendicular to $\overrightarrow{AQ}$. Because those line segments are perpendicular to the same ray, they are all parallel to each other. Therefore, all the right triangles formed are similar. Notice that the sine ratios for angle A, using the similar triangles, are all equivalent. The same is true for the cosine and tangent ratios.

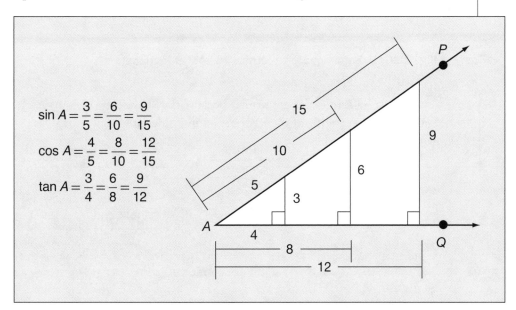

Fig. 3.29. Example showing that similar right triangles yield equivalent trigonometric ratios

Students will learn in later grades how to find an angle measure, given a trigonometric ratio for that angle. For example, using a trig table or a calculator, they will find that the acute angle whose sine is 3/5 is approximately

36.87 degrees. So the measure of angle A in figure 3.29 is approximately 36.87 degrees.

Students further connect their understanding of triangles and the Pythagorean theorem as they learn about special triangles—the 45°-45°-90° triangle and the 30°-60°-90° triangle. One reason these triangles are considered special is that each type is "half" of a familiar polygon; a 45°-45°-90° triangle is "half" of a square and a 30°-60°-90° triangle is "half" of an equilateral triangle.

Students can use the relationship of these triangles to their corresponding familiar polygon to learn more about their properties. For example, the diagonal of any square is the hypotenuse of a 45°-45°-90° triangle, as illustrated in figure 3.30 for a square whose sides are 1 unit long. According to the Pythagorean theorem, the diagonal d of the square has length $\sqrt{2}$ units as shown. So if the legs of a 45°-45°-90° triangle have length 1 unit, then the length of the hypotenuse is $\sqrt{2}$ units, or about 1.414 units.

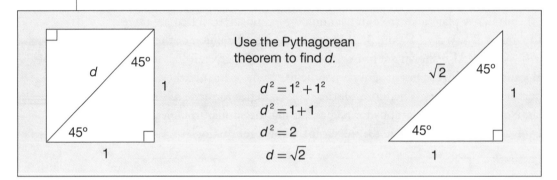

Fig. 3.30. Using a square to form a 45°-45°-90° triangle

All 45°-45°-90° triangles are similar because they have the same angle measures, thus the lengths of their corresponding sides are proportional, as shown in figure 3.31.

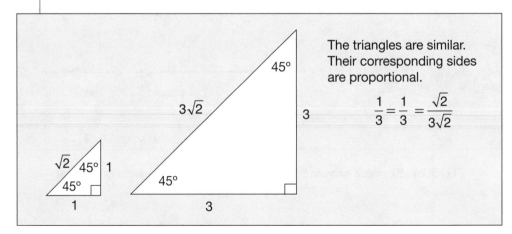

Fig. 3.31. All 45°-45°-90° triangles are similar.

The side lengths of the small triangle in figure 3.31 are 1, 1, and $\sqrt{2}$. The side lengths of the large triangle are 3, 3, and $3\sqrt{2}$. In general, the side lengths of any 45°-45°-90° triangle are a, a, and $a\sqrt{2}$, where a is the length of each congruent leg and $a\sqrt{2}$ is the length of the hypotenuse.

Students can also learn about the 30°-60°-90° triangle by looking at its corresponding equilateral triangle. As illustrated in figure 3.32, an altitude (a line drawn from one vertex perpendicular to the opposite side) in an equilateral triangle forms two congruent triangles, each with angle measures 30 degrees, 60 degrees, and 90 degrees. Students can use the Pythagorean theorem to find that if the sides of an equilateral triangle are 2 units long, then the altitude h has length $\sqrt{3}$ units. So if the legs of a 30°-60°-90° triangle have lengths 1 unit and $\sqrt{3}$, or about 1.732, units, then the length of the hypotenuse is 2 units.

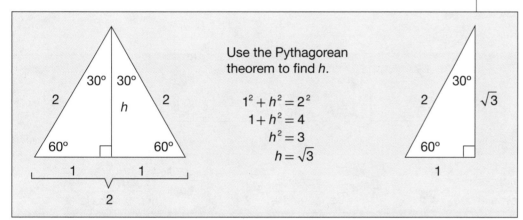

Fig. 3.32. Using an equilateral triangle to form a 30°-60°-90° triangle

All 30°-60°-90° triangles are similar because they have the same angle measures; thus the lengths of the corresponding sides of any two 30°-60°-90° triangles are proportional, as in the example in figure 3.33.

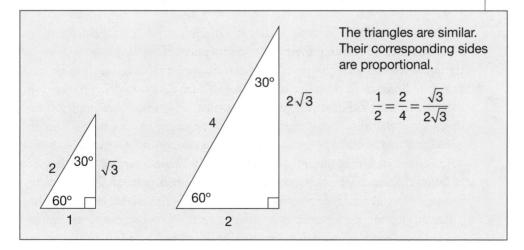

Fig. 3.33. All 30°-60°-90° triangles are similar.

The side lengths of the small triangle in figure 3.33 are 1, $\sqrt{3}$, and 2. The side lengths of the large triangle are 2, $2\sqrt{3}$, and 4. In general, the side lengths of any 30°-60°-90° triangle are a, $a\sqrt{3}$, and $2a$, where a is the length of the short leg, $a\sqrt{3}$ is the length of the long leg, and $2a$ is the length of the hypotenuse.

Because all 45°-45°-90° triangles are similar, any 45°-45°-90° triangle can be used to write trigonometric ratios for 45 degrees. And because all 30°-60°-90° triangles are similar, any 30°-60°-90° triangle can be used to write trigonometric ratios for 30 degrees and 60 degrees. Figure 3.34 shows the sine, cosine, and tangent ratios for 45 degrees, 30 degrees, and 60 degrees.

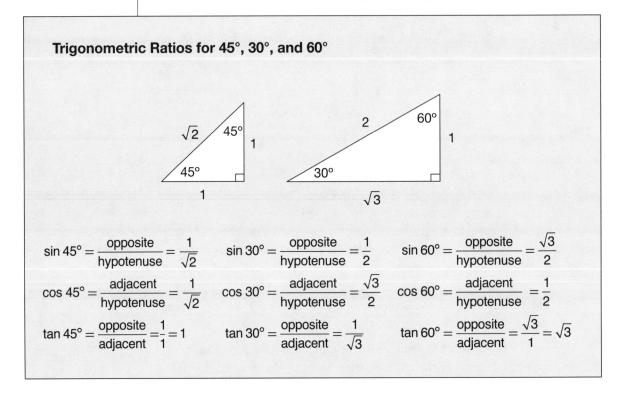

Trigonometric Ratios for 45°, 30°, and 60°

$$\sin 45° = \frac{\text{opposite}}{\text{hypotenuse}} = \frac{1}{\sqrt{2}} \qquad \sin 30° = \frac{\text{opposite}}{\text{hypotenuse}} = \frac{1}{2} \qquad \sin 60° = \frac{\text{opposite}}{\text{hypotenuse}} = \frac{\sqrt{3}}{2}$$

$$\cos 45° = \frac{\text{adjacent}}{\text{hypotenuse}} = \frac{1}{\sqrt{2}} \qquad \cos 30° = \frac{\text{adjacent}}{\text{hypotenuse}} = \frac{\sqrt{3}}{2} \qquad \cos 60° = \frac{\text{adjacent}}{\text{hypotenuse}} = \frac{1}{2}$$

$$\tan 45° = \frac{\text{opposite}}{\text{adjacent}} = \frac{1}{1} = 1 \qquad \tan 30° = \frac{\text{opposite}}{\text{adjacent}} = \frac{1}{\sqrt{3}} \qquad \tan 60° = \frac{\text{opposite}}{\text{adjacent}} = \frac{\sqrt{3}}{1} = \sqrt{3}$$

Fig. 3.34. Trigonometric ratios for the acute angles in special right triangles

Students will also learn to connect their understanding of the properties of triangles, including the sum of the measures of a triangle, to explore the properties of other polygons. Students discover that diagonals can be drawn to decompose polygons into triangles. This allows students to develop a deeper understanding of the properties of the polygons. For example, if students know that the sum of the measures of the angles in a triangle is 180 degrees, and that another polygon can be decomposed into four triangles, they can reason that if they multiply the number of triangles, four, by 180, they will find the sum of the measures of the angles in that polygon. Furthermore, through carefully crafted experiences with triangles formed by vertices of the polygon, students can observe that the interior of a polygon can be separated into two fewer triangles than its number of sides; thus, a quadrilateral is composed of 4 – 2 = 2 triangles, a pentagon is composed of 5 – 2 = 3 triangles, a hexagon is composed of 6 − 2 = 4 triangles, and so on. Students learn to connect these patterns with the algebraic representations that they have learned to write this relationship algebraically as "the sum of the angles in a polygon with n sides = $(n − 2)180$." Students then can use this expression to find the sum of the measures of the angles in any polygon, as shown in figure 3.35.

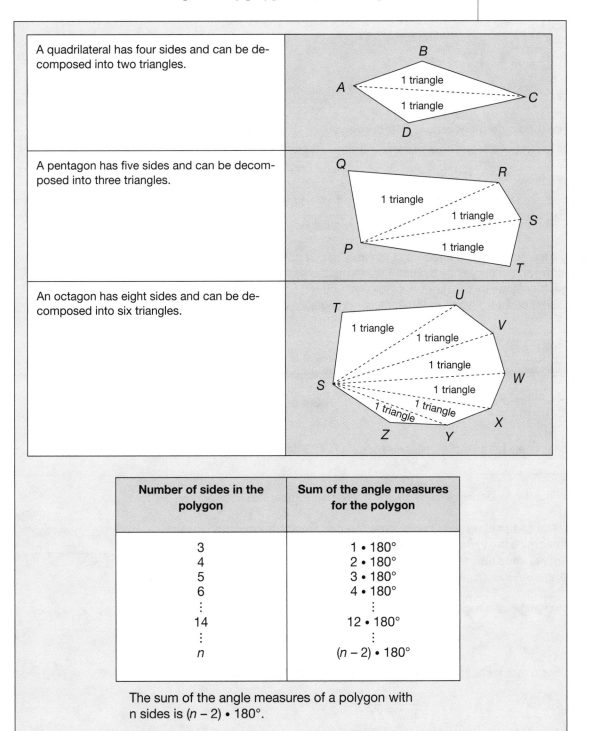

Number of sides in the polygon	Sum of the angle measures for the polygon
3	1 • 180°
4	2 • 180°
5	3 • 180°
6	4 • 180°
⋮	⋮
14	12 • 180°
⋮	⋮
n	$(n − 2)$ • 180°

The sum of the angle measures of a polygon with n sides is $(n − 2)$ • 180°.

Fig. 3.35. Sum of the measures of the angles of a polygon

Students can apply these understandings to solve problems involving polygons and discover other angle properties and relationships in polygons. Some of these problems and properties are summarized in figure 3.36.

Problem: Find the missing angle measure in the polygon.

Solution: The polygon has five sides, so $n = 5$.

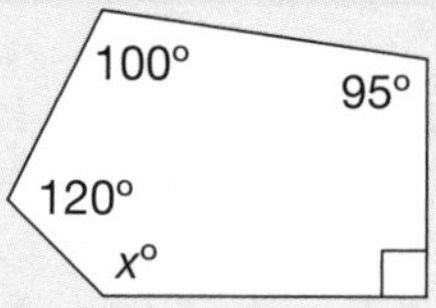

$$(n - 2) \bullet 180° = (5 - 2) \bullet 180° = 3 \bullet 180° = 540°$$

The sum of the angle measures is 540 degrees.

$$x + 120 + 100 + 95 + 90 = 540$$
$$x + 405 = 540$$
$$x = 135$$

The missing angle measure is 135 degrees.

Problem: Find the measure of each angle in a regular hexagon.

Property: If the sum of the measures of the angles in a polygon is $(n - 2)180$, and in a regular polygon the angles all have the same measure, then if you divide the sum of the angle measures by the number of angles, you will find the measure of each angle. So the measure of each of the angles in a regular polygon is

$$\frac{(n - 2)180}{n}.$$

Solution: For example, a regular hexagon has six angles, so $n = 6$.

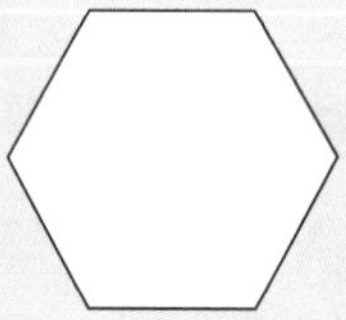

$$\frac{(n - 2)180}{n} = \frac{(6 - 2)180}{6} = \frac{4(180)}{6} = \frac{720}{6} = 120$$

The measure of each angle of a regular hexagon is 120 degrees.

Problem: Find the measure of each central angle of a regular hexagon.

Property: The center of a regular polygon is the point inside the polygon that is equidistant from all the vertices. The center of this hexagon is P. A central angle is an angle whose vertex is the center and whose sides contain two consecutive vertices. Angle APB is a central angle. A regular polygon with n sides has n central angles whose sum is 360 degrees. These angles are all congruent, so the measure of the central angle of a regular polygon is

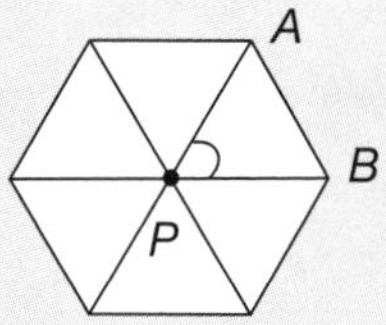

$$\frac{360°}{n}.$$

Solution: For a regular hexagon, the measure of each central angle is

$$\frac{360°}{6} = 60°.$$

Fig. 3.36. Problems students can solve about the angles in polygons

Students can also apply their understanding of angles to discover properties of the exterior angles in a polygon. An exterior angle of a polygon is formed by extending a side, such as this:

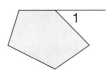

At each vertex of a polygon there are two exterior angles and, since they are vertical angles, they are congruent.

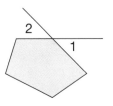

Through activities such as the one shown in figure 3.37, students learn that the sum of one of each of the exterior angles at each vertex of a polygon is 360 degrees and that an exterior angle and its adjacent interior angle are supplementary.

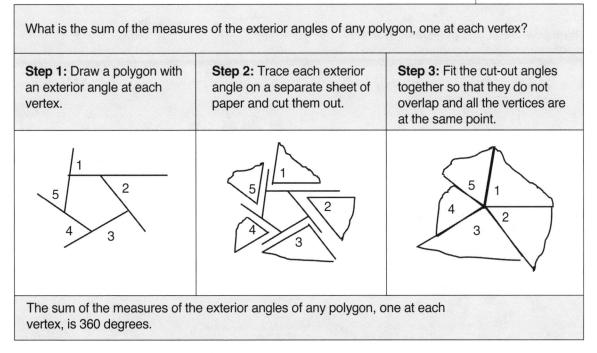

What is the sum of the measures of the exterior angles of any polygon, one at each vertex?		
Step 1: Draw a polygon with an exterior angle at each vertex.	**Step 2:** Trace each exterior angle on a separate sheet of paper and cut them out.	**Step 3:** Fit the cut-out angles together so that they do not overlap and all the vertices are at the same point.

The sum of the measures of the exterior angles of any polygon, one at each vertex, is 360 degrees.

Fig. 3.37. Activity exploring the exterior angles of a polygon

Connections in later grades

In grade 8, students are laying the foundation for many of the more sophisticated concepts they will learn in later grades. For example, students' work with congruence and similarity will be applied when students learn about the various combinations of conditions that ensure congruent and similar triangles, such as the postulates and theorems shown in figures 3.38 and 3.39.

Note that although the first four of these statements about congruent triangles are presented as postulates, there is a theorem that says the four statements are equivalent, so there is really only one assumption that can appear in four different settings.

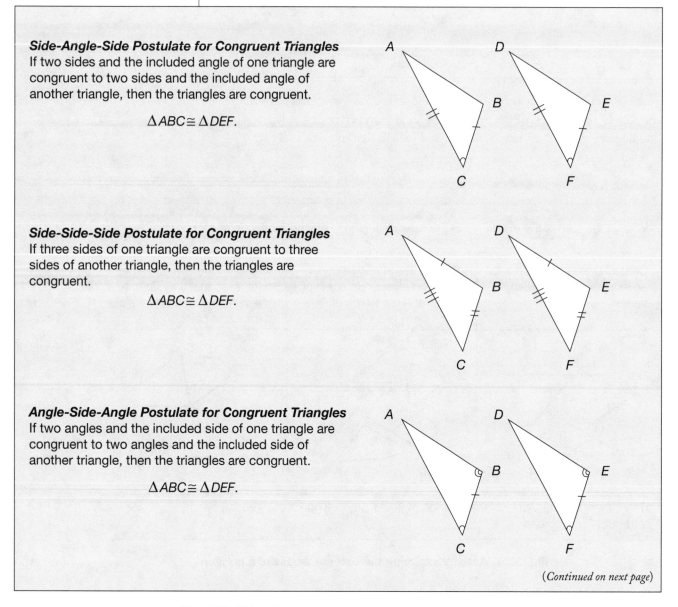

Side-Angle-Side Postulate for Congruent Triangles
If two sides and the included angle of one triangle are congruent to two sides and the included angle of another triangle, then the triangles are congruent.

$$\triangle ABC \cong \triangle DEF.$$

Side-Side-Side Postulate for Congruent Triangles
If three sides of one triangle are congruent to three sides of another triangle, then the triangles are congruent.

$$\triangle ABC \cong \triangle DEF.$$

Angle-Side-Angle Postulate for Congruent Triangles
If two angles and the included side of one triangle are congruent to two angles and the included side of another triangle, then the triangles are congruent.

$$\triangle ABC \cong \triangle DEF.$$

(*Continued on next page*)

Fig. 3.38. Triangle congruence postulate and theorems

Angle-Angle-Side Postulate for Congruent Triangles
If two angles and a nonincluded side of one triangle are congruent to two angles and a nonincluded side of another triangle, then the triangles are congruent.

$\triangle ABC \cong \triangle DEF$.

Hypotenuse-Leg Theorem of Congruent Triangles
If the hypotenuse and a leg of one right triangle are congruent to the hypotenuse and a leg of another right triangle, then the triangles are congruent.

$\triangle ABC \cong \triangle DEF$.

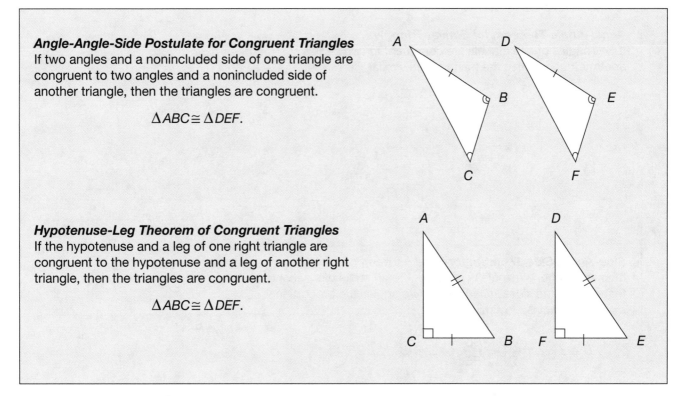

Fig. 3.38. Triangle congruence postulate and theorems—*Continued*

Students learn that since two polygons are similar if and only if all their corresponding pairs of angles are congruent *and* all their corresponding pairs of side lengths are proportional, then to maintain the system of Euclidean geometry, the postulate that states that similar triangles can be determined if the three pairs of corresponding angles are congruent, that is, the proportionality of the sides does not have to also be known, is accepted as true. This postulate, the angle-angle-angle postulate for similar triangles, provides the necessary conditions to prove the other theorems listed in figure 3.39.

Angle-Angle-Angle Postulate for Similar Triangles
If three angles of one triangle are congruent to three angles of another triangle, then the triangles are similar.

$\triangle ABC \sim \triangle DEF$.

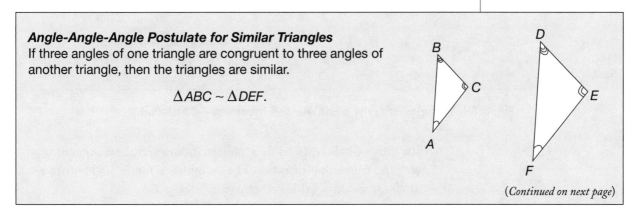

(*Continued on next page*)

Fig. 3.39. Triangle similarity postulate and theorems

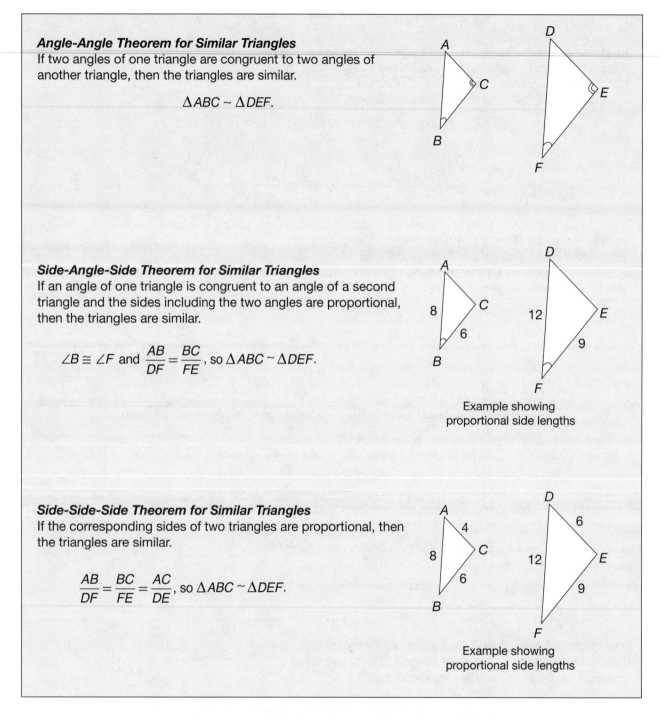

Angle-Angle Theorem for Similar Triangles
If two angles of one triangle are congruent to two angles of another triangle, then the triangles are similar.

$$\triangle ABC \sim \triangle DEF.$$

Side-Angle-Side Theorem for Similar Triangles
If an angle of one triangle is congruent to an angle of a second triangle and the sides including the two angles are proportional, then the triangles are similar.

$$\angle B \cong \angle F \text{ and } \frac{AB}{DF} = \frac{BC}{FE}, \text{ so } \triangle ABC \sim \triangle DEF.$$

Example showing proportional side lengths

Side-Side-Side Theorem for Similar Triangles
If the corresponding sides of two triangles are proportional, then the triangles are similar.

$$\frac{AB}{DF} = \frac{BC}{FE} = \frac{AC}{DE}, \text{ so } \triangle ABC \sim \triangle DEF.$$

Example showing proportional side lengths

Fig. 3.39. Triangle similarity postulate and theorems—*Continued*

Students will also expand their understanding and application of trigonometry and trigonometric ratios. The examples in figure 3.40 illustrate how students will apply this knowledge in later grades.

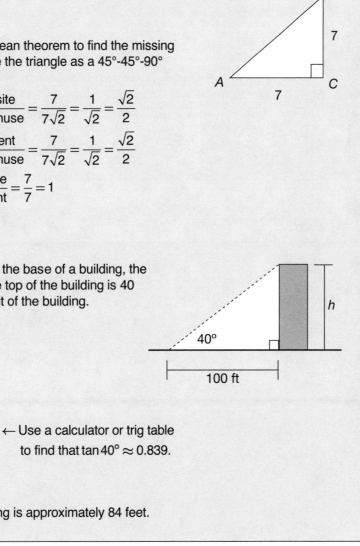

Problem:

Find sin A, cos A, tan A, and $m\angle A$.

Solution:

Either use the Pythagorean theorem to find the missing side length or recognize the triangle as a 45°-45°-90° triangle. $AB = 7\sqrt{2}$

$$\sin A = \frac{\text{opposite}}{\text{hypotenuse}} = \frac{7}{7\sqrt{2}} = \frac{1}{\sqrt{2}} = \frac{\sqrt{2}}{2}$$

$$\cos A = \frac{\text{adjacent}}{\text{hypotenuse}} = \frac{7}{7\sqrt{2}} = \frac{1}{\sqrt{2}} = \frac{\sqrt{2}}{2}$$

$$\tan A = \frac{\text{opposite}}{\text{adjacent}} = \frac{7}{7} = 1$$

$$m\angle A = 45°$$

Problem:

At a point 100 feet from the base of a building, the angle of elevation to the top of the building is 40 degrees. Find the height of the building.

Solution:

Use the right triangle.

$$\tan 40° = \frac{h}{100}$$

$$100(\tan 40°) = h \qquad \leftarrow \text{Use a calculator or trig table}$$
$$\text{to find that } \tan 40° \approx 0.839.$$

$$100(0.839) \approx h$$

$$83.9 \approx h$$

The height of the building is approximately 84 feet.

Fig. 3.40. Examples of how students apply trigonometric concepts in later grades

Developing Depth of Understanding

What activities can you do in your classroom that will help students understand and apply the concept and properties of similarity? What everyday examples can you give to students to show why it is important to be able to use distances and angles to analyze geometric figures and space?

4 Focusing on Analyzing and Summarizing Data Sets

In grade 8, students learn how to analyze and summarize data sets. Students learn how to choose the appropriate graph to display data and the most meaningful numbers to describe measures of center and spread. They also learn how to display and interpret bivariate data (a data set with two variables) using scatter plots. The goal of this Focal Point is for students to use data and graphs to solve problems.

Instructional Progression for Analyzing and Summarizing Data Sets

The focus on analyzing and summarizing data sets in grade 8 is supported by a progression of related mathematical ideas before and after grade 8, as shown in table 4.1. To give perspective to the grade 8 work, we first discuss some of the important ideas that students focus on before grade 8 that prepare them for learning how to analyze and summarize data sets in grade 8. At the end of the detailed discussion of this grade 8 Focal Point, we present examples of how students will use analyzing and summarizing data sets in later grades. For more detailed discussions of the "before" part of the instructional progression, please see the appropriate grade-level books, for example, *Focus in Grade 6* (NCTM 2010) and *Focus in Grade 7* (NCTM 2010).

Early Foundations for Analyzing and Summarizing Data Sets

Students have learned many mathematical concepts and skills prior to grade 8 that lay the foundation for their ability to analyze and summarize data sets in grade 8. In grades 3 through 5, students collect and organize data, often using tally charts and frequency tables. They learn to display their organized data in various ways, including the use of line plots, bar graphs, picture graphs, stem-and-leaf plots, double-bar graphs, histograms, and line graphs. Students apply their understandings of whole numbers, fractions, and decimals as they display the data in the various forms. They also use various representations of data to solve problems, draw conclusions, and make predictions.

Table 4.1
Grade 8: Focusing on Analyzing and Summarizing Data Sets—Instructional Progression for Analyzing and Summarizing Data Sets

Before Grade 8	Grade 8	After Grade 8
Students apply their understandings of whole numbers, fractions, and decimals to construct frequency tables, bar graphs, picture graphs, line plots, stem-and-leaf plots, double-bar graphs, and line graphs.*	Students use their knowledge of data displays to represent data in a variety of ways and compare the representations in order to make an informed decision about which representation to use for a given set of data.	Students formulate questions that can be addressed with data and collect, organize, and display relevant data to answer them.
Students use these various representations of data to solve problems.*	Students find, use, and interpret measures of center (mean, median, and mode) to summarize and analyze data.	Students select and use appropriate statistical methods to analyze data.
Students develop an understanding of proportional relationships.	Students find, use, and interpret measures of spread (range, quartiles, outliers) to summarize and analyze data.	Students develop and evaluate inferences and predictions that are based on data.
Students use proportions to make estimates relating to a population on the basis of a sample.**	Students use data displays, measures of center, and measures of spread to develop and create and evaluate inferences and predictions related to the data.	Students understand and apply basic concepts of probability.
Students apply percentages to make and interpret histograms and circle graphs.**		

* In Grades 3–5 Connections
** In Grade 7 Connections

In grade 7, students use proportions to make estimates relating to a population on the basis of a sample. For example, they might use proportions to analyze the following situation:

Suppose 200 taxpayers in a town are randomly selected for a survey and 120 of them are in favor of using tax money to build a new school. On the basis of the random survey, if there are 5,000 taxpayers in the town, about how many of the taxpayers in the town might you expect to be in favor of using tax money to build a new school?

Students would set up and solve the proportion

$$\frac{120}{200} = \frac{x}{5,000},$$

finding that $x = 3,000$. So one could expect that about 3,000 taxpayers in the town would be in favor of using tax money to build a new school.

In grade 7, students also learn how to apply percents to make and interpret circle graphs. For example, suppose sixty students are asked to name the subject in which they are getting the best grade; fifteen name science, fifteen name mathematics, eighteen name social studies, and twelve name language arts. They could determine that 15 is 25% of 60, 18 is 30% of 60, and 12 is 20% of 60. Next they could calculate that $0.25 \times 360° = 90°$, $0.30 \times 360° = 108°$, and $0.20 \times 360° = 72°$. Finally, they could use their results to make a circle graph, as shown in figure 4.1.

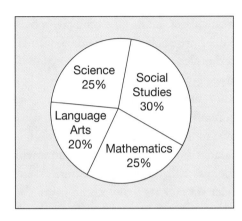

Fig. 4.1. Circle graph made by students using percents

In grade 8, students will synthesize this prior knowledge to create new knowledge as they further expand their ability to analyze and summarize data sets.

Focusing on Analyzing and Summarizing Data Sets

The focus of analyzing and summarizing data sets in grade 8 is on evaluating the strengths and weaknesses of different data displays, learning that descriptive statistics provide additional information that can be used to analyze data, and understanding that ways exist to study the strength of the association of two sets of data. Throughout the work related to this Focal Point, students should encounter learning experiences that are contextual. Also, as students study data analysis, they should compare sets of data that are slightly different. As students observe how differences in data affect the shape of a graph, as illustrated in a data display, and the descriptive statistical values that are associated with the data, their understanding of data analysis deepens. In addition to working with data provided for them, students should also be given the opportunity to collect, display, and analyze their own data.

Creating and comparing different data displays

In grade 8, students further develop their ability to understand the strengths and weaknesses of different data displays. They learn to articulate which data displays are best for which types of data. For students to gain this ability, they need opportunities to interpret data displays, as well as create data displays from given data sets. As students create, interpret, discuss, and compare a variety of data displays for data sets of different types, they develop the ability to make informed decisions about which representation or representations are suitable to use for a given set of data. Classroom discussions like the one that follows give students the opportunity to create, discuss, and compare data displays.

Teacher: Look at the list of scores on a quiz taken by twenty students in a mathematics class. When we analyze a set of data, we make summary statements about it. For example, we might summarize quiz data by saying that most of the class did well on the quiz, or most of the class did poorly. We might say that a certain number of people got the same score, or that no one got the same score. There are many different ways that we could analyze a set of data so that it is meaningful to us if we know enough about the details of the context that the data came from. Look at the following quiz scores. The highest grade possible was 100, and this is the quiz given at the end of a unit. Are there any summary statements that you can make about the data?

70	70	80	80	95	65	65	82	82	77
85	95	95	100	100	70	77	85	55	75

Jorge: It seems like there were both high and low grades. There seem to have been a lot of grades in the 80s, but I can't really tell unless I count them all.

Teacher: Jorge's observations are correct. When we look at a list of numbers, it can be difficult to analyze the list because it is difficult to see patterns. You have learned other ways to show these data. Can anyone tell me some other ways that we might display this set of data rather than in a list?

Mia: Yes; we could use a table or a graph.

Teacher: Mia has mentioned some other ways to display these data that might make it easier to analyze. One of the purposes of graphing data is to give you a *picture* of the data. This picture can make it easier to analyze and summarize the data. Now make a data display to show these data another way. Be sure your display has a title and that you label your graph as necessary.

Teachers would then allow students to display the data in any way they wish. The purpose of this open exploration is to give students the opportunity to make data displays as well as to compare data displays. Through this process, students begin to see that there are often different ways to display data and that, depending on what we need to learn about the data, some ways of displaying data are more useful than others. In these initial experiences with choosing their own data displays, students are likely to choose data displays with which they have had previous experiences. These previous experiences may vary, but students are likely to have previous experience with bar graphs, line graphs, line plots (dot plots), stem-and-leaf plots, circle graphs, histograms, and pictographs. Once students have made their data displays, teachers should allow them to explain their data displays, including why they chose them, and encourage them to evaluate the relative strengths and weaknesses of the displays, as reflected in the continuation of the classroom discussion that follows.

Teacher: I see that different students created different types of displays for this data set. Elivo, will you please share your graph?

Elivo: I made a bar graph. First I wrote the data values in order: 55, 65, 65, 70, 70, 70, 75, 77, 77, 80, 80, 82, 82, 85, 85, 95, 95, 95, 100, 100. Then I grouped together all the grades in the 50s, 60s, 70s, 80s, 90s, and 100. Then I used bars to show the number of students that got grades in each group.

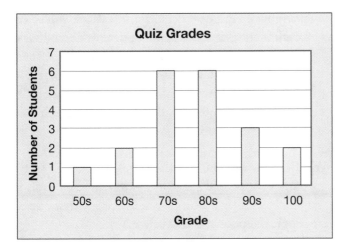

Teacher: How does your graph make it easier to analyze the data, Elivo?

Elivo: Well, I can see that most of the people got grades in the 70s and 80s. I can see that the fewest people got grades in the 50s and 100; also, that the same number of people got grades in the 70s and 80s.

Teacher: Those are good observations, Elivo. Part of accurately displaying data is being sure that the intervals are all the same. Does anyone see a problem with the intervals in Elivo's graph?

Mia: I do. All the intervals include ten numbers, except the 100. That is only one number. I think it makes the graph a little bit misleading because two people got scores in the 60s, and two people got 100, but on the graph this is represented the same way.

Teacher: Good observation, Mia. Since Elivo's intervals do not each represent the same number of scores, his graph could be misleading.

Frank: I made a graph with bars, but I think mine more accurately displays the data. I used intervals that are equal on my graph. Every bar represents ten possible grades, and the bars touch because there is no gap between one interval and another.

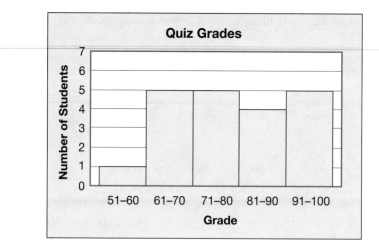

Teacher: Frank made a histogram, which is a graph that uses bars to show frequencies of data grouped in intervals. His intervals are indeed equal, and the frequency of each interval is the number of data values in that interval. An advantage of a histogram is that it gives a good idea of the shape of the distribution, or arrangement, of numerical data. If you compare Elivo's graph and Frank's graph, you can see that the shapes of the graphs are different. Since Frank's graph uses equal intervals, the shape of his graph more accurately shows a "picture" of the data. What analysis can you make from your graph, Frank?

Frank: Well, I can see that most of the scores are from 71 to 100 and that about the same number of people got scores in the three intervals from 71 to 100. By this graph, it seems that most people did pretty well on the quiz and that only a few people did poorly, or got below a 70.

Teacher: Frank's comments illustrate the reason we display data in an organized way. It is easier to analyze the set of data when data are displayed than when they are just in a list. Having a picture of the data helps you make more accurate summary statements about the data. One characteristic of a histogram that might be a disadvantage, depending upon what you want to know about the data, is that it does not show the actual data values. For example, you cannot tell from looking at the graph how many students got 100, or whether the scores in the 60s were above or below 65. Beth, I see that you did not use bars to make a graph. Can you share your graph?

Beth: I made a line graph. First I wrote the data values in order, then I grouped them into equal intervals, and then plotted the number of scores in each group.

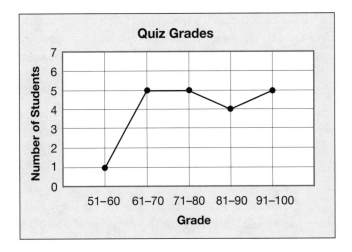

Teacher: Beth used points and lines rather than bars to show her data. A line graph is usually used to display changes over time, to show trends, or to show a relationship between two variables. This data set is a list of quiz scores. Beth, do you think any of these purposes of a line graph are needed for this set of data?

Beth: I guess not. The quiz data do not show change over time or any kind of trend. It is just showing how many scores are in each group. Maybe I should have made a bar graph like Frank, since the lines between the points don't really mean anything. I think if the data were something like one student's twenty quiz scores, it might be better to use a line graph, because you could show a trend in that person's scores, for example, whether the person's scores went down, improved, or stayed about the same.

Teacher: Della, you made an interesting data display. Can you share it with the class?

Della: My graph is different from the ones everyone has shared so far because it shows every data point. This might make it easier to interpret the data because you can see, for example, how many 100s there are. My graph is a little like a bar graph or histogram, but it uses x-marks instead of bars. The number of each data value is shown by that number of x-marks instead of by the height of a bar.

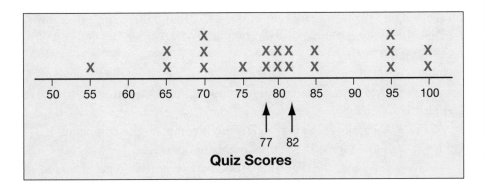

Teacher: Della's graph is called a line plot. It also can be called a dot plot because sometimes dots are used instead of x-marks. Della described one of the advantages of a line plot—that it shows all the actual data values. Can anyone see a limitation of Della's display?

Della: Yes; I am limited by the scale on the number line. If, for example, my data ranged from 0 to 2,000 and I had to fit this range onto the page, then data points close to one another, like 1,344 and 1,345, would be difficult to show accurately. Also, if I had more data points, for example 100 or 200 quiz scores, it would take quite a bit of time to make the plot without some help, like from a computer.

Teacher: Della's observations are accurate. As we are beginning to see, there are disadvantages and advantages of the different kinds of graphs. Some of these advantages and disadvantages are based on the type of data you are displaying and some are characteristics of the data display itself.

Teacher: Carmen, you made an interesting graph. Can you share it?

Carmen: I made a circle graph. Like Frank, I first wrote the data values in order. But I grouped them into slightly different groups, as you can see on my graph.

Quiz Grades

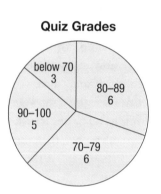

Teacher: How did you determine the sizes of the sectors in your graph?

Carmen: Well, for example, I wrote 3 scores out of 20 scores as 3/20, then I found 3/20 of 360°:

$$\frac{3}{20} \cdot 360° = \frac{3}{20} \cdot \frac{360°}{1} = \frac{3}{\cancel{20}} \cdot \frac{\cancel{360°}\ 18°}{1} = 54°.$$

So the section for the 3 scores below 70 is 54°. I found these angle measures for the other sections the same way: 108° for 70–79, 108° for 80–89, and 90° for 90–100.

Teacher: How is your graph different from all the others that we have seen?

Carmen: Well, my graph is a circle. Also it compares the number of grades in each category with the total number of grades.

Teacher: You can make that comparison between the amount of data in a category and the amount of data in the whole set with most of the graphs we've seen, but a circle graph is especially good for displaying data in distinct categories as parts of a whole. A circle graph usually uses categories to organize data. When the data items are numbers, such as these quiz scores, and are separated into ordered groups like Carmen's, the groups are called *intervals*. As we have seen in Elivo's graph, when forming intervals, it is usually best to make the intervals the same size. The first interval, below 70, includes all scores from 0 to 69, so it is much larger than the other intervals. What are the sizes of Carmen's other intervals?

Elivo: The 70–79 interval has ten possible scores, the 80–89 interval has ten possible scores, and the 90–100 interval has eleven scores.

Teacher: Normally, you would want to have intervals that are equal so that you can most accurately display the data. Even though the intervals are not equal in Carmen's graph, we can still use it to analyze the data. What is some information we can get from the circle graph?

Carmen: I can see that the number of scores in the 80–89 range was the same as the number of scores in the 70–79 range and that the least number of people got scores below 70. The section for the 90–100 scores seems to be about one-quarter of the circle, so about one-quarter of the people got a score in this range; also the sections show that more than half the students got grades between 70 and 89.

Teacher: Let's look at one more graph. Alex, will you share your graph?

Alex: I made a stem-and-leaf plot. Like a line plot, it shows all the actual data values. I put a key on it so that you could see how to read it.

Quiz Grades

5	5
6	5 5
7	0 0 0 5 7 7
8	0 0 2 2 5 5
9	5 5 5
10	0 0

Key: 8|2 = 82

Teacher: Alex, your plot accurately displays the data. If you turn your plot, you can see that it is like a bar graph, but the "bars" tell you the exact values. Does anyone see limitations of a stem-and-leaf plot?

```
                7     5
                7     5
                5     2
                0     2     5
          5     0     0     5     0
    5     5     0     0     5     0
   ─────────────────────────────────
    5     6     7     8     9     10
```

Della: I do; they are similar to a line plot. It would be difficult to show many values, for example, 100 values. Also, if the values had a big range, like from 0 to 3,000, it would be inefficient to show them in this way.

Teacher: Well, at least without the use of technology it would be more difficult.

Reflect As You Read

The class discussion in the previous section revealed a class in which students were able to make many different graphs for one set of data. Examine the work of your own students. Do they come with the same background exhibited by students in the previous discussion? What do your students understand about the characteristics of each type of graph?

Through classroom discussions such as the previous one about many different types of data sets, students learn that some displays are more appropriate for some types of data and some are more appropriate for other types of data. They also learn that for many data sets, several types of data displays may be appropriate, as illustrated in figure 4.2. The circle graph and bar graph both show data in distinct categories, and they are both good for comparing the amounts in the categories. The circle graph offers the additional advantage of making it easy to compare the amount in each category to the whole.

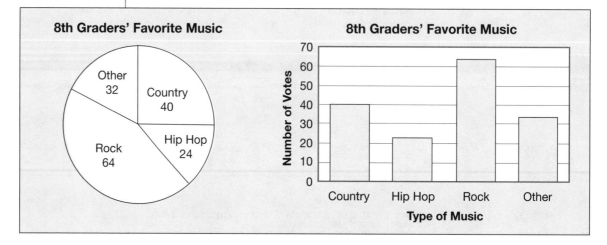

Fig. 4.2. Circle graph and bar graph

During classroom discussions, students should also have the opportunity to compare and contrast bar graphs and histograms. Through various experiences making and interpreting these two types of graphs, they should realize that both graphs use bars to show the frequency of each group and neither graph shows the actual data values. They should also realize that histograms are used to display continuous data grouped in intervals, whereas in bar graphs, separated bars are used to represent discrete data grouped in different categories. Students should gain an appreciation that stem-and-leaf plots and line plots are useful when wanting to show actual data values, showing extremes, clustering, outliers, and range but are best suited for data sets that have forty or fewer data values.

Students may also see the commonalities among some of the data displays. For example, a bar graph, line graph, histogram, line plot, and stem-and-leaf plot all give a "picture" of the data, so they provide a good idea of the shape of the distribution. Although some of these displays also provide actual data values, others use length or area to show frequency.

As students learn more about using different types of data displays, they learn that often two sets of data can be graphed on one display, for example, on a double-line graph, a double-bar graph, or a double stem-and-leaf plot. Graphing more than one set of data on one display allows students to compare the data quickly, as shown in figure 4.3. By a glance at the single-bar graph, the students can be compared by grade; by a glance at the double-bar graph, boys and girls in each grade can be compared.

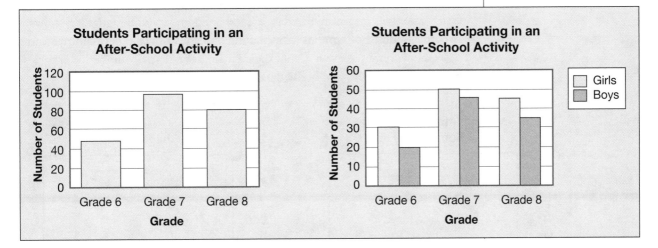

Fig. 4.3. Single-bar graph and double-bar graph showing data from same data set

Bar graphs can also be horizontal, as shown in figure 4.4.

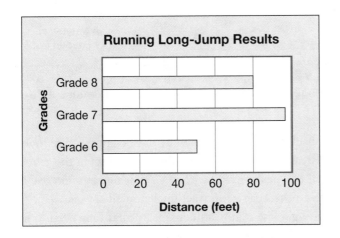

Fig. 4.4. Horizontal bar graph

107

During their work with data displays, students learn that line graphs are useful when they want to show changes over time, trends, and the relationship between two variables. Data represented in a line graph can be either discrete or continuous. For discrete data, only certain values are possible, and those values are often, but not always, whole numbers. Some examples of discrete data are number of people in a family, number of stores in a shopping mall, and shoe size (which may have a limited number of fractional values). For continuous data, the number of possible values between any two data values is infinite. This does not mean there are an infinite number of values in a data set. Rather, the term *continuous data* refers to the nature of the quantity being measured or recorded. A good example of continuous data is a person's height. As a girl grows from 40 inches tall to 41 inches tall, she grows gradually, attaining heights such as 40 1/2 inches, 40 13/16 inches, 40 29/32 inches, and so on. Not every height between 40 inches and 41 inches can be measured or recorded, but growth is continuous because there are no gaps from one fraction of an inch to another. Other examples of continuous data are age and temperature. Figure 4.5 shows two line graphs. Both graphs show a trend and a relationship between two variables. However, in the first graph, the data are discrete (i.e., number of participants). In the second graph, the data are continuous (i.e., height).

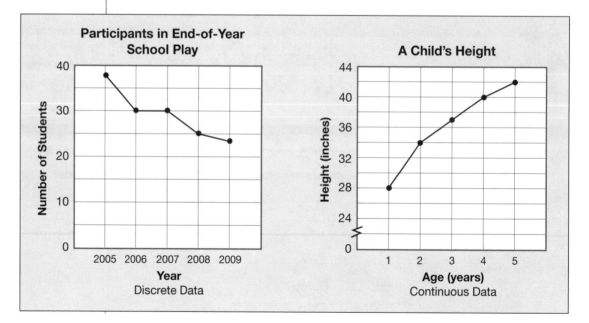

Fig. 4.5. Line graphs representing discrete data and continuous data

Referring back to figure 4.5, it would also be appropriate to use dashed lines rather than solid lines to connect the data points in the school-play graph. The dashed lines emphasize the fact that there are no real data between the data points, that is, no fractional students.

When reading a line graph, students learn that they need to interpret several aspects of the graph. First, they have to determine if the data are discrete or continuous—do fractional values make sense in the given context?

They also have to understand which data points were actually measured and if there are meaningful data between those data points. For example, in figure 4.6, two temperature line graphs are given. As students learn to analyze the data between the data points, they come to realize that in graph B, the line might or might not approximate the data that could have been collected between the existing data points. For example, when the temperature changes from 53°F to 56°F between 2:00 p.m. and 3:00 p.m., the line that shows that the temperature gradually increased is probably a fairly accurate representation of the actual change in temperature between the two times. However, in graph A, the line between 8:00 p.m. on Thursday and 8:00 p.m. on Friday probably does not accurately represent the actual change in temperature over time. There were probably much greater fluctuations between these two data points than indicated by the line. As students learn to analyze line graphs, it is important that they learn to make these types of inferences from the context within which the data are situated.

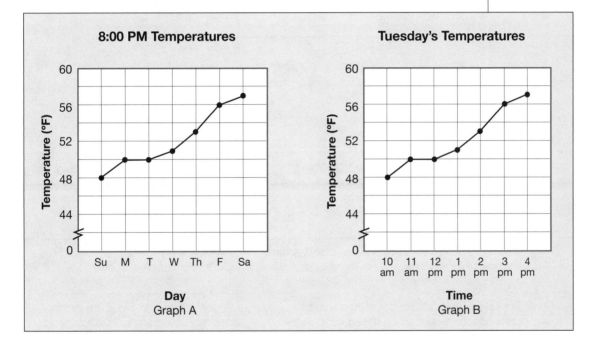

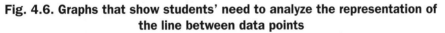

Fig. 4.6. Graphs that show students' need to analyze the representation of the line between data points

Students also learn about double-line graphs and use them to compare trends in data, as shown in figure 4.7. Notice that in this case, the dashed line is used to differentiate between the two restaurants. Neither restaurant has actual data between the days.

Information about different displays that students are likely to have previously encountered is summarized in figure 4.8.

Once students have developed the ability to decide which display is appropriate for certain data and they can create and interpret different displays, teachers should begin to ask such questions as these:

- How can you identify a single number that is representative of the whole set of data?

- How can you identify a single number that describes the spread of the data?

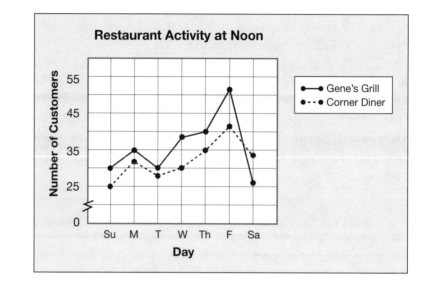

Fig. 4.7. Double-line graph

Type of Display	Strengths/Advantages/Utility	Weaknesses/Disadvantages
Line graph	Used to display changes over time; shows trends; used to show the relationship between time and another variable.	Care must be taken to interpret the segments connecting actual data points.
Circle graph	Displays data in distinct categories; displays data as parts of a whole; good for comparing and contrasting the relative amounts in the categories.	Useful for relative frequency; does not show trends or behavior over time.
Bar graph	Displays data in distinct categories; good for comparing and contrasting the amounts in the categories.	Categories are often not in any order; data must be interpreted appropriately.
Histogram	Good for displaying data that can be grouped into ordered intervals; gives a good idea of the shape of the distribution.	Does not show actual data values.
Line plot	Good way to show extremes, clustering, outliers, and range; shows actual data values.	Not good when there are many data values or when the range of the data values is great.
Stem-and-leaf plot	Helps you see how data are distributed; shows actual data values; helps you see repeated data values and other patterns.	Not good when there are many data values or when the range of the data values is great.
Pictograph	Helps you quickly compare differences in numerical data.	Often shows approximate instead of actual data values.

Fig. 4.8. Data displays students have likely encountered before grade 8

As students search for answers to these questions, they begin to realize that the answers are not easily found in their data displays or in the data sets themselves. This realization provides teachers with the opportunity to introduce the purpose of studying descriptive statistics, which includes measures of center, spread, and distribution.

Measures of center

In grade 8, students find, use, and interpret measures of center to summarize and analyze data. These measures include mean, median, mode, and midrange. The purpose of identifying a measure of center is to choose a single number, or representative value, that represents an entire data set. Students may be familiar with the term *average* as another name for measure of center. Average is used because the measure of center can be thought of as a "normal" or "typical" value in the data set. This term, however, can be misleading because it is often used interchangeably with *mean*; for example, the phrase "average speed" is usually used to refer to the mean speed and the phrase "average temperature" is used to refer to the mean temperature. Additionally, the mode is sometimes not considered to be a measure of center; however, it is a *representative* or *typical* member of a data set, one of the characteristics of a measure of center.

The mean of a data set is the sum of the values in the data set divided by the number of values. Students should understand a mean as a fair-share measure as well as a balance point (Franklin et al. 2007). It is beneficial for students to explore the concept of the mean through concrete experiences before they use addition and division to compute the mean. Examples of different ways to model the mean are shown in figure 4.9.

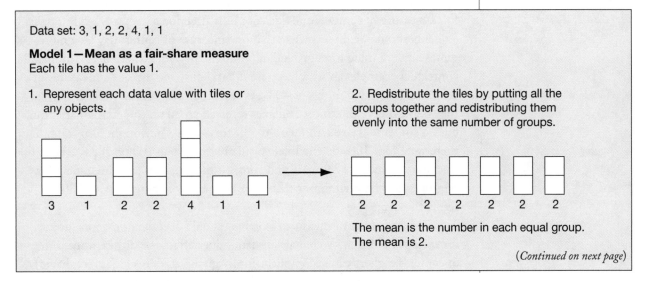

Data set: 3, 1, 2, 2, 4, 1, 1

Model 1—Mean as a fair-share measure
Each tile has the value 1.

1. Represent each data value with tiles or any objects.

2. Redistribute the tiles by putting all the groups together and redistributing them evenly into the same number of groups.

3   1   2   2   4   1   1

2   2   2   2   2   2   2

The mean is the number in each equal group.
The mean is 2.

(*Continued on next page*)

Fig. 4.9. Modeling mean

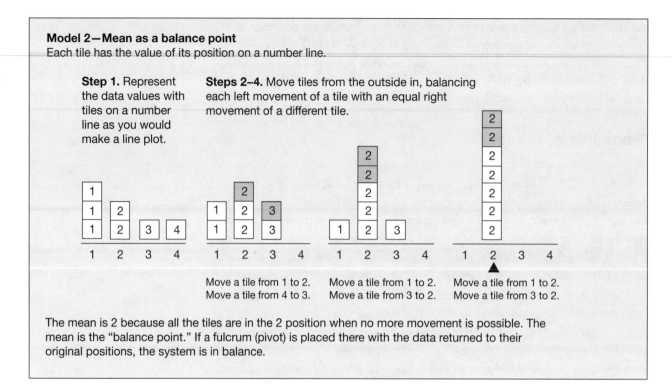

Model 2—Mean as a balance point
Each tile has the value of its position on a number line.

Step 1. Represent the data values with tiles on a number line as you would make a line plot.

Steps 2–4. Move tiles from the outside in, balancing each left movement of a tile with an equal right movement of a different tile.

Move a tile from 1 to 2.
Move a tile from 4 to 3.

Move a tile from 1 to 2.
Move a tile from 3 to 2.

Move a tile from 1 to 2.
Move a tile from 3 to 2.

The mean is 2 because all the tiles are in the 2 position when no more movement is possible. The mean is the "balance point." If a fulcrum (pivot) is placed there with the data returned to their original positions, the system is in balance.

Fig. 4.9. Modeling mean—*Continued*

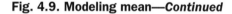

Figure 4.10 shows the definitions of mean and other measures of center along with some examples.

As students begin exploring measures of center and other descriptive statistics, teachers should carefully craft learning experiences to give students the opportunity to discover that although measures of center are often very useful, a measure of center alone does not fully describe a data set. Additionally, students should begin to realize that one measure of center may be a more representative value for a given data set than another. Experiences can include contextual examples in which different data sets have the same measures of center, as illustrated in figure 4.11. As students analyze the two sets of data, they may observe that most students received an 80 on the mathematics quiz but no student received an 80 on the history quiz. They might also state that there were four 100s on the history quiz but only one 100 on the mathematics quiz. As students compare and contrast the data sets and line plots, they reinforce in their own minds that these measures of center do not fully describe the data.

Students' study of measures of center should also include opportunities for them to realize how changes in data values affect the different measures of center. Teachers can accomplish this by giving students a data set, having them find its measures of center, and then purposefully changing the data set so that students can analyze how a particular change affected the measures of center as shown in figures 4.12, 4.13, and 4.14.

Definitions of measures of center of a data set

The *mean* is the sum of the values divided by the number of values.

The *median* is the middle value when the values are written in numerical order. If the number of values is even, the median is the mean of the two middle values.

The *midrange* is the mean of the extremes.

The *mode* is the value that occurs most often. A data set can have no mode (that is, there is no data value that occurs more than once), one mode, or more than one mode. Mode is actually sometimes considered a representation of distribution rather than a measure of center.

Examples

Data Set	Measures of Center
2, 6, 8, 8, 4	Mean: $\dfrac{2+6+8+8+4}{5} = \dfrac{28}{5} = 5.6$ Median: Write the data values in order and then identify the middle value: 2 4 <u>6</u> 8 8. The median is 6. (Half of the data are above 6; half are below 6.) Midrange: The extremes are 2 and 8. Midrange $= \dfrac{2+8}{2} = 5$. Mode: The mode is 8.
4, 0, 1, 0, 9, 7, 7, 8	Mean: $\dfrac{4+0+1+0+9+7+7+8}{8} = \dfrac{36}{8} = 4.5$ Median: Write the data values in order. The number of values is even. Identify the two middle values. 0 0 1 <u>4 7</u> 7 8 9 Find the mean of the two middle values. $\dfrac{4+7}{2} = \dfrac{11}{2} = 5.5$ The median is 5.5. (Half of the data are above 5.5; half are below 5.5.) Midrange: The extremes are 0 and 9. Midrange $= \dfrac{0+9}{2} = \dfrac{9}{2} = 4.5$. Mode: The modes are 0 and 7.

Fig. 4.10. Definitions and examples of different measures of center

The original data set given in figure 4.12 is characterized by having a cluster of values in the middle of the set and the same number of values above and below that cluster. Through their completion of many activities with data sets having these characteristics, students begin to see that when values are added to the lower end of a data set such as this, the mean decreases; when values are added to the upper end of the data set, the mean increases; and when values are added to the middle of a data set, the mean stays about the same. They can also surmise that when there is a cluster of data in the middle of the data set, when values are added to the lower and upper end, the median may not be affected.

Data Sets:
60, 70, 70, 80, 80, 80, 80, 90, 90, 100   60, 60, 60, 60, 70, 90, 100, 100, 100, 100

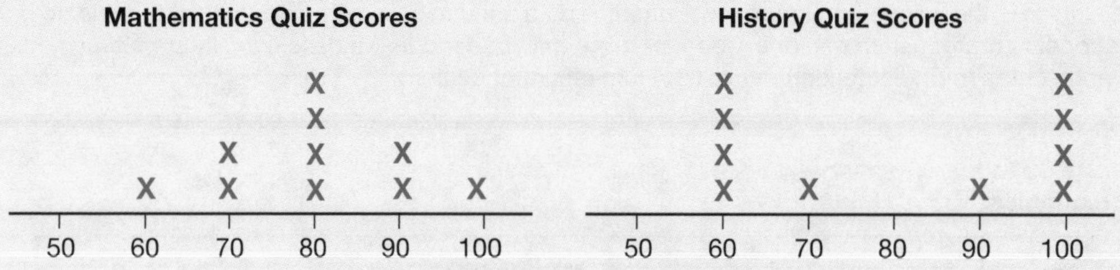

Mathematics Quiz Scores   **History Quiz Scores**

	Scores on Quizzes	
	Mathematics Quiz	History Quiz
Mean	80	80
Median	80	80
Midrange	80	80

Fig. 4.11. Different data sets with the same measures of center

Set A

1. Original data set:

70, 80, 80, 80, 90

Mean = 80

Median = 80

Mode = 80

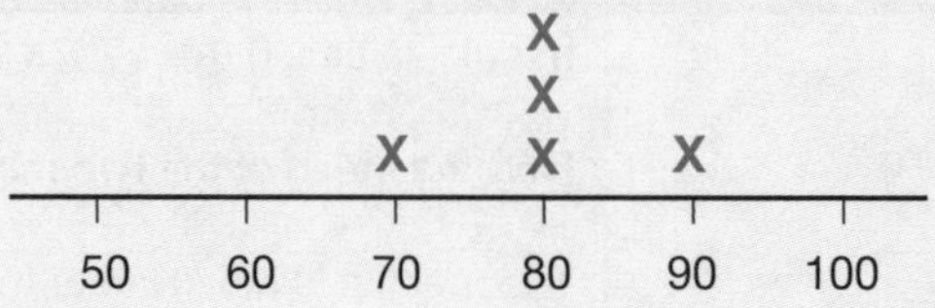

The mean, median, and mode are all the same.

The graph is symmetric, with the value of the measures of center, 80, in the middle.

2. Add 60 to the original data set:

60, 70, 80, 80, 80, 90

Mean = $76\frac{2}{3}$

Median = 80

Mode = 80

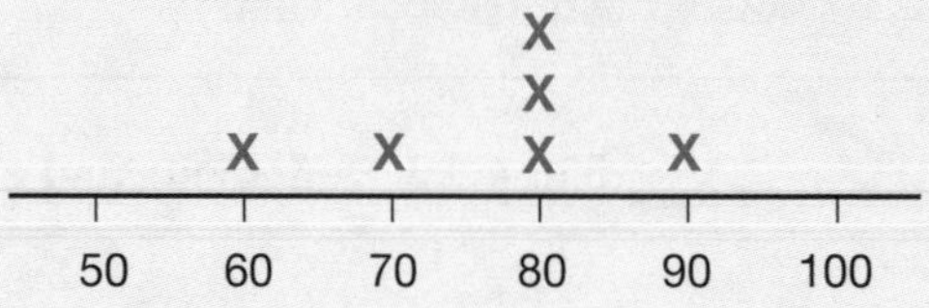

The new data value, 60, was added to the lower end of the data set.

The mean decreased; the median and mode are the same.

The graph is no longer symmetric; it is stretched out somewhat to the left.

(Continued on next page)

Fig. 4.12. Activity 1—comparing the effects of additional data on measures of center

3. Add 100 to the original data set:

70, 80, 80, 80, 90, 100

Mean = $83\frac{1}{3}$

Median = 80

Mode = 80

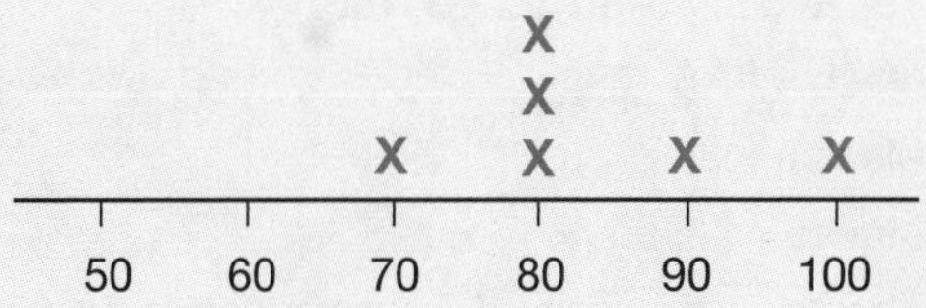

```
                              X
                              X
                    X    X    X    X
          ┬────┬────┬────┬────┬────┬
          50   60   70   80   90   100
```

The new data value, 100, was added to the upper end of the data set.

The mean increased; the median and mode are the same.

The graph is no longer symmetric; it is stretched out somewhat to the right.

4. Add 80 to the original data set:

70, 80, 80, 80, 80, 90

Mean = 80

Median = 80

Mode = 80

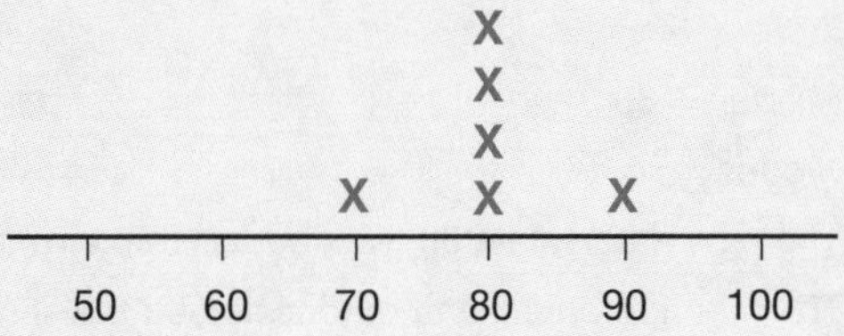

```
                              X
                              X
                              X
                    X    X    X
          ┬────┬────┬────┬────┬────┬
          50   60   70   80   90   100
```

The new data value, 80, was added to the middle of the data set.

The mean, median, and mode stayed the same.

The graph is still symmetric, with more values in the center.

Fig. 4.12. Activity 1—comparing the effects of additional data on measures of center—*Continued*

Set B

1. Original data set:

70, 70, 70, 80, 90, 90, 90

Mean = 80

Median = 80

Modes = 70, 90

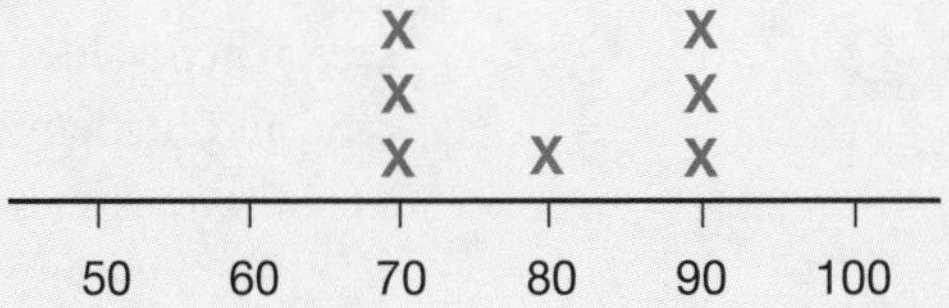

```
                    X         X
                    X         X
                    X    X    X
          ┬────┬────┬────┬────┬────┬
          50   60   70   80   90   100
```

The mean and median are the same.

There are two modes, 70 and 90. The graph is symmetrical around 80.

2. Add 60 to the original data set:

60, 70, 70, 70, 80, 90, 90, 90

Mean = 77.5

Median = 75

Modes = 70, 90

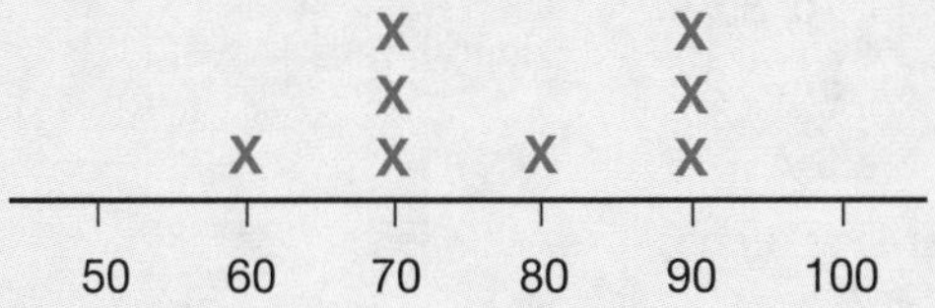

```
                    X         X
                    X         X
               X    X    X    X
          ┬────┬────┬────┬────┬────┬
          50   60   70   80   90   100
```

The new data value, 60, was added to the lower end of the data set.

The mean and median decreased; the modes are the same.

The graph is stretched out somewhat to the left.

(*Continued on next page*)

Fig. 4.13. Activity 2—comparing the effects of additional data on measures of center

3. Add 100 to the original data set:

70, 70, 70, 80, 90, 90, 90, 100

Mean = 82.5

Median = 85

Modes = 70, 90

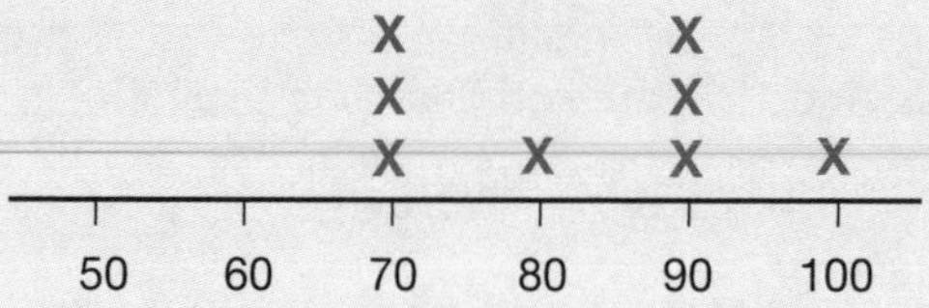

```
                                    X           X
                                    X           X
                                    X   X   X   X
        +---+---+---+---+---+---+
        50  60  70  80  90  100
```

The new data value, 100, was added to the upper end of the data set.

The mean and median increased; the modes are the same.

The graph is stretched out somewhat to the right.

4. Add 80 to the original data set:

70, 70, 70, 80, 80, 90, 90, 90

Mean = 80

Median = 80

Modes = 70, 90

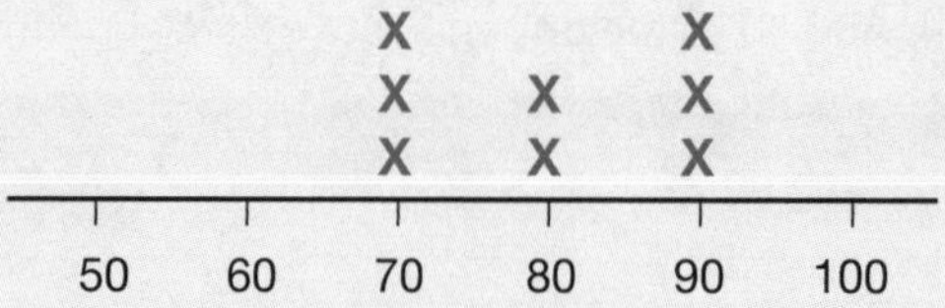

```
                                    X           X
                                    X   X   X
                                    X   X   X
        +---+---+---+---+---+---+
        50  60  70  80  90  100
```

The new data value, 80, was added to the middle of the data set.

The mean, median, and modes stayed the same.

The graph is perfectly symmetric, like the original graph, with 80 in the middle and high at the modes, 70 and 90. It is just slightly higher in the middle at 80 than the original graph.

Fig. 4.13. Activity 2—comparing the effects of additional data on measures of center—*Continued*

The original data set given in figure 4.13 is characterized by having a cluster of values at the lower end, a cluster of values at the upper end, and few values in the middle of the data set. Through their completion of many activities with data sets having these characteristics, students begin to see that when values are added to the lower end of a data set such as this, the mean and median decrease; when values are added to the upper end of the data set, the mean and median increase; and when values are added to the middle of the data set, the mean and median stay about the same.

Set C

1. Original data set:

50, 70, 80, 90

Mean = 72.5

Median = 75

Mode: none

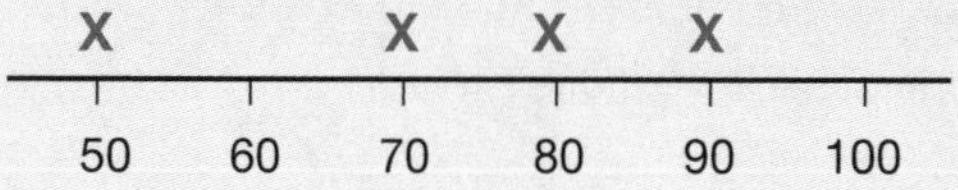

```
        X           X   X   X
        +---+---+---+---+---+---+
        50  60  70  80  90  100
```

The mean and median are different. There is no mode.

The graph is not symmetric; all columns are the same height.

(*Continued on next page*)

Fig. 4.14. Activity 3—comparing the effects of additional data on measures of center

2. Add 50 to the original data set:

50, 50, 70, 80, 90

Mean = 68

Median = 70

Mode: 50

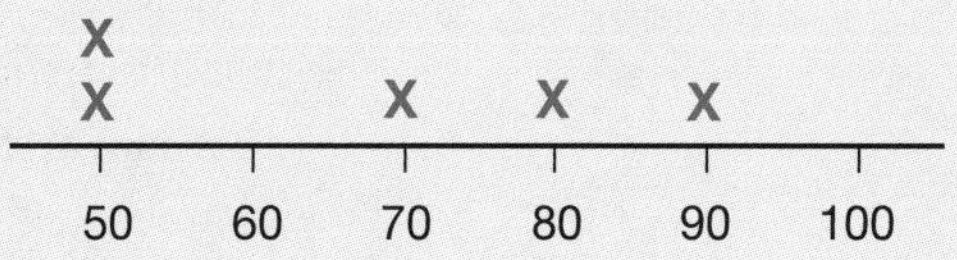

```
X
X          X    X    X
|----|----|----|----|----|
50   60   70   80   90   100
```

The new value, 50, was added to the low end of the data set.

The mean and median decreased, and now there is a mode.

The graph is still not symmetric; now the tallest column is at the low end of the data.

3. Add 100 to the original data set:

50, 70, 80, 90, 100

Mean = 78

Median = 80

Mode: none

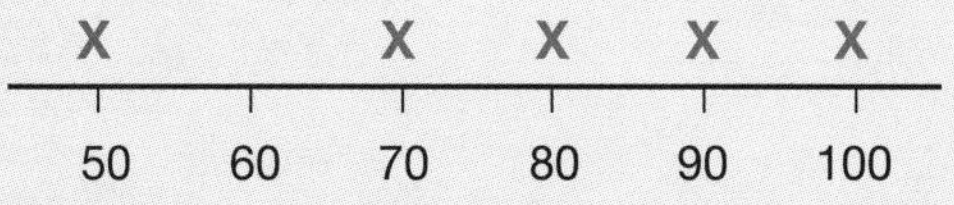

```
X          X    X    X    X
|----|----|----|----|----|
50   60   70   80   90   100
```

The new value, 100, was added to the upper end of the data set.

The mean and median increased, and there is still no mode.

The graph is still not symmetric; all columns are the same height.

4. Add 80 to the original data set:

50, 70, 80, 80, 90

Mean = 74

Median = 80

Mode: 80

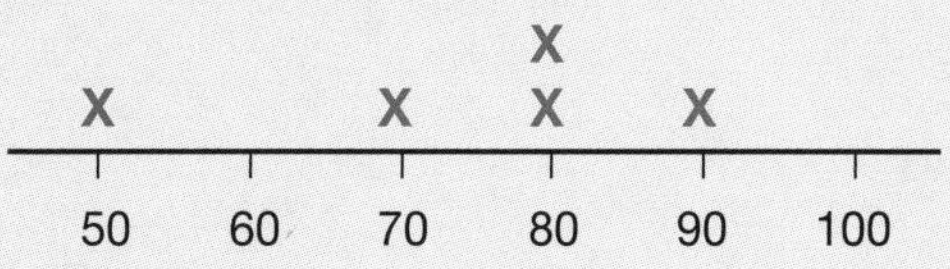

```
                    X
X          X    X    X
|----|----|----|----|----|
50   60   70   80   90   100
```

The new value, 80, was added to the middle of the data set.

The mean increased, the median stayed the same, and there is now a mode.

The graph is still not symmetric; now the tallest column is near the middle of the data.

Fig. 4.14. Activity 3—comparing the effects of additional data on measures of center—*Continued*

The original data set given in figure 4.14 is characterized by not having a cluster of values; all the values have about the same occurrence. Through their completion of many activities with data sets having these characteristics, students begin to see that when values are added to the lower end of a data set such as this, the mean and median decrease and, if the added value is already in the set, the mode changes. When values are added to the upper end of the data set, the mean and median increase, and if the added value is already in the set, the mode changes. When values are added to the middle of a data set, the mean and median may or may not be affected. It depends on whether the new value is exactly in the middle of the values or is less or greater than the middle values. If the added value is already in the set, the mode changes.

Figure 4.15 provides a summary of generalizations about the shape of a data distribution, measures of center, and how measures of center and a distribution shape are affected by changes in data that students should be able to make after many experiences with adding data to data sets with different characteristics.

- **If a data set is symmetric about a data value, then that value is the mean and median.**
- **If a data value is inserted in the low end of a data set, then—**
  - the mean decreases.
  - the median might decrease.
  - the mode is not affected unless the inserted data value becomes a mode.
  - if the shape of the original graph is symmetric, then the shape of the new graph is not symmetric, with another value to the left of the original center.
- **If a data value is inserted in the high end of a data set, then—**
  - the mean increases.
  - the median might increase.
  - the mode is not affected unless the inserted data value becomes a mode.
  - if the shape of the original graph is symmetric, then the shape of the new graph is not symmetric, with another value to the right of the original center.
- **If a data value is inserted in the middle of a data set, then—**
  - the mean and median may or may not be affected, but the change will be minimal.
  - the mode is not affected unless the inserted data value becomes a mode.
  - if the shape of the original graph is symmetric, then the shape of the new graph will still be symmetric or somewhat symmetric.

Fig. 4.15. Summary of how changes in data affect measures of center

After students have several experiences finding measures of center and analyzing the effect that changes in different types of data sets have on these measures, they are ready to begin evaluating whether all measures of center are equally reflective of the data in every context. Students begin to realize that they need to make decisions about which measures of center best represent certain data and begin gaining the ability to describe situations in which a particular measure of center would be more reflective of the data than another. Students also learn that in certain situations, measures of center can be misleading.

Whether a measure of center is reflective of a data set is based on the context in which that data set is generated. Because of this, teachers should construct a series of purposeful, contextual experiences in which students can first observe and then determine the most appropriate measure of center. Problems such as the ones provided in the following classroom discussion give students these opportunities.

Teacher: Let's look at some problems and decide if all measures of center accurately reflect a representative value for the set of data or if one measure of center is more appropriate to use than another. Suppose the following numbers represent a student's ten mathematics quiz scores. What are the mean, median, and mode?

90	100	100	70	90
100	100	70	80	70

Barry: The grades in order from least to greatest are 70, 70, 70, 80, 90, 90, 100, 100, 100, 100. The mean is 870/10 = 87; the median is 90; the mode is 100.

Teacher: Each of these measures has a different value. Which measure of center do you think best represents the data?

Ayaan: I think the mean best represents the data because it seems to be most like the student's overall performance. Although the student got the most 100s, he or she also got grades much lower than 100, so the mode is not as good. The middle grade, the median, is 90, but some of the student's grades are much lower than 90 (for example, he got three 70s), so the 90 seems too high to represent all the grades. I think the mean, as a balance point, is the best value to use to describe this data.

Teacher: You provided logical support for your reasoning. Let's look at another data set. Suppose your family owns a grocery store. You sell cereal in 12-ounce, 16-ounce, 20-ounce, and 24-ounce boxes. You make the same amount of profit on each size. The data values below are ounces, showing the last 20 boxes you sold. Find the mean, median, and mode of the data.

12	16	12	16	16	24	20	12	20	12
16	12	20	12	24	12	20	24	12	24

Cheryl: The order of the data from least to greatest is 12, 12, 12, 12, 12, 12, 12, 12, 16, 16, 16, 16, 20, 20, 20, 20, 24, 24, 24, 24. The mean is 336/20 = 16.8; the median is 16; and the mode is 12.

Teacher: Now suppose a supplier offers a discount on the next shipment if you order all boxes of the same size. If your family decides to take advantage of the offer, which measure of center should your family use to determine the best size to order?

Jim: I think my family should use mode. The data indicates that we sell more of that size than any other size. The mean is 16.8, and you can't order a 16.8-ounce size because it is not available. It makes most sense in this case to order the size box that people buy most often, which is the mode, 12.

Teacher: I understand your reasoning, Jim. So in the case of the grades, the mean was the most appropriate measure of center to use, but in the case of the cereal boxes, it was the mode. Let's look at another situation. Suppose a company placed this advertisement in a magazine.

Career Opportunities!
Established Company
Representative Salary: $68,000

The company has nine employees, including the vice-president and president. These are their salaries. What are the mean, median, and mode of the salaries?

$35,000 $35,000 $35,000 $40,000 $40,000
$42,000 $42,000 $143,000 $200,000

Janie: The mean is $612,000/9 = $68,000; the median is $40,000; and the mode is $35,000.

Teacher: Those measures of center are correct. Is the advertisement truthful?

Jim: Well, the advertisement is not untruthful because the mean is $68,000, and the mean is a measure of center, and so it is a representative value of the salaries. You could say that it is the average salary of the people who work at the company.

Gladys: Well, I think that saying that $68,000 is a representative salary might be technically true, but it is misleading. The mean of the salaries is raised because of the vice-president's and president's salaries, which are much greater than the other employees' salaries. If you get a job with this company, it is likely that you will get a salary that is much lower than $68,000. I think that the median, $40,000, would be more representative of the data set, in that it would give someone applying a more accurate idea of how much they might make if they got the job.

Teacher: Jim and Gladys bring up important points. Jim's point shows us that it is possible for measures of center to be intentionally or unintentionally misleading. Gladys emphasizes that you need to look carefully at the data and the measures of center before you use measures of center to make decisions or draw conclusions. In some cases, such as this one, the median might be a more representative value than the mean. Let's look at one last data set. The points a basketball player scored in ten games are these:

5   6   8   8   8   10   10   11   11   12

What are the mean, median, and mode of the data?

Kimberly: The mean is 89/10 = 8.9; the median is 9; and the mode is 8.

Teacher: Kimberly, which measure of center best represents the player's contribution to the team?

Kimberly: Well, in this case, all the measure-of-center values are about the same. I would say that you could use any of them.

Teacher: Good observation, Kimberly. Sometimes the measures of center have about the same value, so any of them can be considered representative of the data set.

As students are given the opportunity to explore and discuss many different situations that involve a variety of data sets, they will gain the ability to describe types of situations in which one measure of center is more appropriate to use than another.

Measures of spread

As students continue their exploration of descriptive statistics, they learn that the use of measures of center is only one way to summarize and analyze data. Another way is to use measures of spread, also called *measures of variability*, to indicate how spread out the data values are. To understand these measures, students need to know about extremes, clusters, and outliers.

Extremes are the least value, or minimum, and the greatest value, or maximum, in a data set. A cluster forms when many values in a data set are close together. As shown in figure 4.16, clusters can be identified on data displays and in lists of numbers that have been ordered.

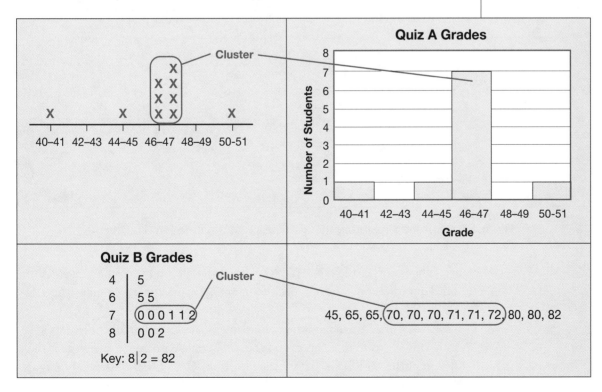

Fig. 4.16. Data displays and lists of data that show clusters

An outlier is a value that is much greater or much less than most of the other values in the set. In the data sets that students will consider in grade 8, outliers are the extreme values. In later grades, however, students will participate in more in-depth outlier analysis that may result in outliers not being included in data representations and descriptive statistics (Franklin et al. 2007).

In grade 8, students learn about two measures of spread: *range* and *interquartile range*. The range of data is the difference between the two extremes, the maximum value minus the minimum value. For example, for the following set of quiz scores—

60 70 76 76 76 80 80 80 80 80 82 82 85 86 86 88 88 90 90 100

the minimum is 60, the maximum is 100, and

range = maximum − minimum = 100 − 60 = 40.

To find the interquartile range, students need to understand how to separate the data into four parts. In this procedure, students apply their understanding of median as the middle of an ordered data set. The median separates the data set into two halves: the lower half and the upper half. Students learn that if they then find the median of the lower half of the data and the median of the upper half of the data, they have divided the whole data set into four parts, or quartiles (*quart*—meaning four), as shown in figure 4.17.

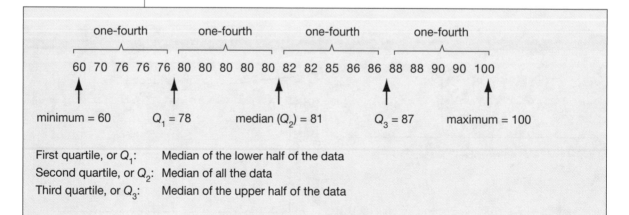

Fig. 4.17. Quartiles separating the distribution of the data into fourths

The interquartile range (*IQR*) is the difference between the first and third quartiles. So, referring back to figure 4.17, interquartile range = $Q_3 − Q_1$ = 87 − 78 = 9.

To summarize, the range is a measure of the spread of an entire data set from minimum to maximum, and the interquartile range is a measure of the spread of the middle half of the data set from Q_1 to Q_3, as illustrated in figure 4.18.

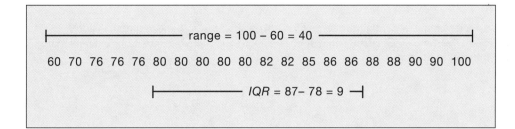

Fig. 4.18. Range and interquartile range (*IQR*) of a data set

Students learn that quartiles divide data into four parts in which approximately one-fourth of the data are below the first quartile, approximately one-fourth of the data are between the first quartile and the median (or the second quartile), approximately one-fourth of the data are between the median and the third quartile, and approximately one-fourth of the data are above the third quartile. The interquartile range, then, incorporates about two-fourths of the data, or about half of the data. However, as will become apparent to students as they expand their study of spread and quartiles, the fourths into which quartiles divide data are not always exactly equal.

Students learn that they can use quartiles and interquartiles to further analyze and summarize data. In students' previous work with data analysis, they have gained an appreciation that it is easier to see patterns in the data when the data are displayed visually rather than as a list of values. Through classroom discussions about this prior knowledge, teachers can guide students to realize that a display that shows a "picture" of the quartile and interquartile information would be a useful aid when analyzing data. After discussions such as these, students are then ready for teachers to introduce the box-and-whisker plot, or a box plot. Students can also learn how to use the five-number summary of the data—the maximum, minimum, median, and first and third quartiles—to make a box-and-whisker plot, as shown in figure 4.19.

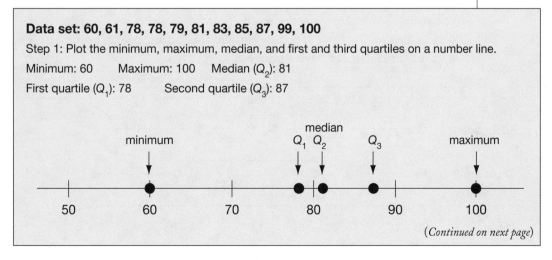

Data set: 60, 61, 78, 78, 79, 81, 83, 85, 87, 99, 100

Step 1: Plot the minimum, maximum, median, and first and third quartiles on a number line.

Minimum: 60   Maximum: 100   Median (Q_2): 81

First quartile (Q_1): 78   Second quartile (Q_3): 87

(*Continued on next page*)

Fig. 4.19. Making a box-and-whisker plot

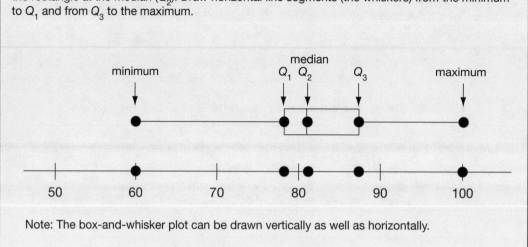

Step 2: Draw a rectangle (the box) from Q_1 to Q_3. Draw a short vertical line segment inside the rectangle at the median (Q_2). Draw horizontal line segments (the whiskers) from the minimum to Q_1 and from Q_3 to the maximum.

Note: The box-and-whisker plot can be drawn vertically as well as horizontally.

Fig. 4.19. Making a box-and-whisker plot—*Continued*

Students can then observe that in a box-and-whisker plot, the lowest fourth of the data are represented by the left whisker, the middle half are represented by the box, and the highest fourth are represented by the right whisker. The box-and-whisker plot in figure 4.19 shows that half of the data are clustered about the median and the rest are widely spread out.

To interpret a box-and-whisker plot, students need to understand that it shows the spread of the data from the minimum to the maximum, which is the range (the entire length of the box and both whiskers). It also shows the "middle spread" about the median, which is the interquartile range (the length of the box). It is evident by comparing the box-and-whisker plots of the data sets shown in figure 4.20 that they have the same minimum, same maximum, same range, and same median. But the greater interquartile range of data set 2 indicates a greater "middle" spread about the median; that is, the data in data set 2 are not as tightly clustered about the median as the data in data set 1; the data are more spread out.

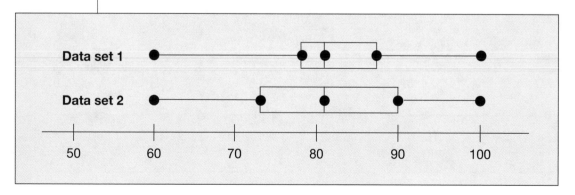

Fig. 4.20. Comparing box-and-whisker plots

Analyzing data on box-and-whisker plots aids in the consideration of the statistical meaning of the data. For example, referring back to figure 4.20, suppose the data sets reflect grades on two different quizzes. The teacher that administered the quiz would make the box-and-whisker plots to summarize the data and learn something about how the students performed on the two quizzes. The teacher can tell from the plots that in data set 2 there is a greater variability of scores in the interquartile range. Although the medians are the same, more students scored lower and more students scored higher on the second quiz.

As students begin to learn how to analyze box-and-whisker plots, it is important that they gain an understanding of what the box and whiskers in the plot represent. For example, they should learn that although one whisker may be longer than another, each whisker in a plot represents about one-fourth of the data and therefore about the same number of values. Also, when comparing two box-and-whisker plots, students need to develop the understanding that a longer box in one graph may or may not represent more data values than a shorter box or whisker in another graph. Both boxes represent about half of the data values; therefore, if there are about the same number of data values in both sets of data, then the longer box indicates that the values are more spread out with respect to the median, and the shorter plot indicates less variability. In a box-and-whisker plot, the length of the box and whiskers indicates the spread of the data, not the size of the data set, as shown in figure 4.21.

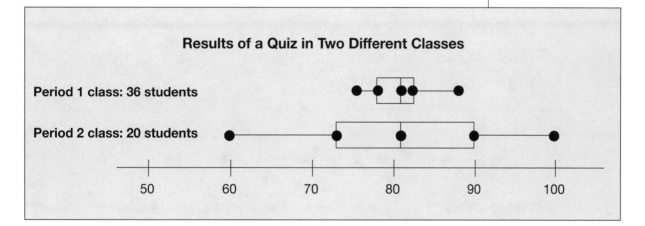

Results of a Quiz in Two Different Classes

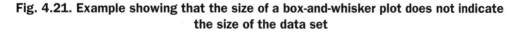

Fig. 4.21. Example showing that the size of a box-and-whisker plot does not indicate the size of the data set

As students begin exploring measures of spread, as with measures of center, teachers should carefully craft learning experiences to give students the opportunity to discover that, although measures of spread are often very useful, a measure of spread alone does not fully describe a data set. Experiences should include contextual examples in which different data sets have the same measure of spread, as illustrated in figure 4.22. Students can be shown the box-and-whisker plots and asked to discuss their measures of spread.

They discover that the measures of spread—the range and the interquartile range—are the same but that the data sets used to create the plots are very different. As students analyze two sets of data, they should observe that although the range and interquartile range are the same in both sets of data, the extremes, median, and first and third quartile values for the data for company A are lower than the corresponding values for company B; thus, although the spread and variability of the salaries in the two companies are the same, the overall salaries in company A are lower than the salaries in company B. As students compare and contrast the box-and-whisker plots, they reinforce in their own minds that these measures of spread, then, do not fully describe the data.

Annual Salaries for Local Companies (in Thousands of Dollars)

Company A

20 20 26 30 30 36 38 38 40 40 40 50 50

Q_1 = \$28,000   median = \$38,000 Q_3 = \$40,000

range = \$50,000 – \$20,000 = \$30,000

interquartile range = \$40,000 – \$28,000 = \$12,000

Company B

30 30 40 44 46 46 46 52 52 54 56 56 60 60 60

Q_1 = \$44,000   median = \$52,000 Q_3 = \$56,000

range = \$60,000 – \$30,000 = \$30,000

interquartile range = \$56,000 – \$44,000 = \$12,000

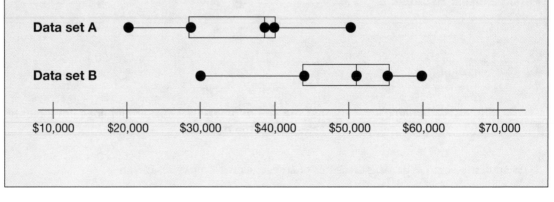

Fig. 4.22. Different data sets with the same measures of spread

As students' understanding of descriptive statistics deepens, they begin to appreciate that each measure contributes to an understanding of the data set and, although the measures of center and spread taken together do not thoroughly describe a data set, together they give a more complete picture of the data than each measure alone.

Reflect As You Read

How well would your students respond to the following prompt?

Given a set of data, create box plots and then write a paragraph about the conclusions that can be drawn. All conclusions should be backed up with data, descriptive statistics, or measures of spread.

As with measures of center, students should be given carefully constructed sets of data values so that they can observe how changes in data values can affect measures of spread. Through class discussions of related sets of data, such as the ones in figure 4.23, students can learn to generalize, then predict, how a change in data values will affect the spread and distribution of the data as shown in a box-and-whisker plot.

Original data set (in thousands of dollars)	Change
	Change one of the $40,000 salaries to $50,000:
20 20 26 30 30 36 38 38 40 40 40 50 50	20 20 26 30 30 36 38 38 40 40 50 50 50
Q_1 = $28,000 median = $38,000 Q_3 = $40,000	Q_1 = $28,000 median = $38,000 Q_3 = $45,000
range = $50,000 – $20,000 = $30,000	range = $50,000 – $20,000 = $30,000
interquartile range: $40,000 – $28,000 = $12,000	interquartile range: $45,000 – $28,000 = $17,000

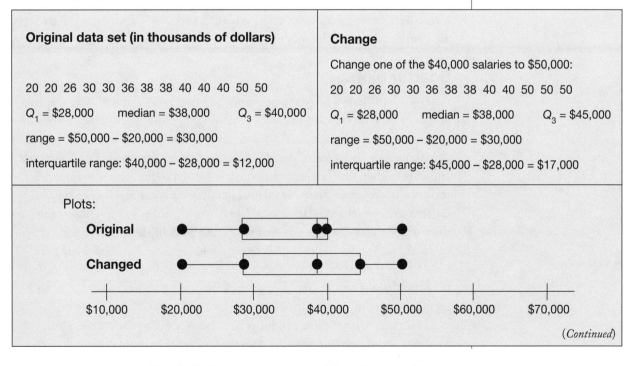

Fig. 4.23. How a change in a data value can affect spread

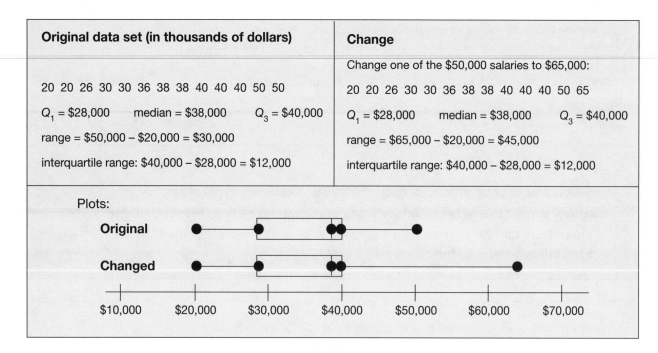

Original data set (in thousands of dollars)	Change
	Change one of the $50,000 salaries to $65,000:
20 20 26 30 30 36 38 38 40 40 40 50 50	20 20 26 30 30 36 38 38 40 40 40 50 65
Q_1 = $28,000 median = $38,000 Q_3 = $40,000	Q_1 = $28,000 median = $38,000 Q_3 = $40,000
range = $50,000 – $20,000 = $30,000	range = $65,000 – $20,000 = $45,000
interquartile range: $40,000 – $28,000 = $12,000	interquartile range: $40,000 – $28,000 = $12,000

Fig. 4.23. How a change in a data value can affect spread—*Continued*

Through guided, structured activities such as the one in figure 4.23, students can learn to generalize that often when data are changed, the quartile in which the change occurs is affected. If extremes are changed, the range and interquartile range may be affected. These changes can affect how the data are distributed about the median.

Scatter plots

After students have had many opportunities to explore familiar data displays and have used descriptive statistics, including measures of center and spread, to summarize data, teachers should begin to ask such questions as "We have the data about quiz scores. We also have data about the number of hours that students studied for the quiz. Suppose we wanted to find out if there was a relationship between these two sets of data. What statistical tools have we learned to explore this relationship?" Teachers should engage in classroom discussions that allow for students' dialogue about all the different kinds of graphs and statistical measures that they have learned and whether they would be sufficient to answer this question. As students discuss the question, they should begin to realize that none of the tools they have learned so far seem adequate to investigate this question.

It is then that teachers can introduce the concept of the scatter plot. Teachers should explain that the data that students have investigated, such as the quiz score data, consist of a set of data involving a single variable, so the data are called single-variable data, or *univariate data*. However, questions such as the one posed about the quiz-score data and the number of hours studying allude to two variables that may possibly be related. A data set involving two variables is called *bivariate data*. To find out if there is a correlation in bivariate data, students learn that they can use a data display called a scatter plot. So, for example, to investigate the question as to whether there is a relationship or correlation between the scores on the quiz and the time spent studying, students can organize the values for the two variables to form a relation of twenty ordered pairs of the form (t, s): (0, 60), (10, 70), and so on, where t is the time each student studied and s is the score that student made on the quiz. Students can then apply what they know about ordered pairs to graph them on a coordinate grid to make a scatter plot, as shown in figure 4.24.

Data about twenty students' scores on the quiz and the time they spent studying:

Student	1	2	3	4	5	6	7	8	9	10
Time (minutes) t	0	10	20	0	10	30	20	20	15	15
Score s	60	70	76	76	76	80	80	80	80	80

Student	11	12	13	14	15	16	17	18	19	20
Time (minutes) t	30	30	35	25	20	35	20	40	40	50
Score s	82	82	85	86	86	88	88	90	90	100

Scatter plot of the relationship:

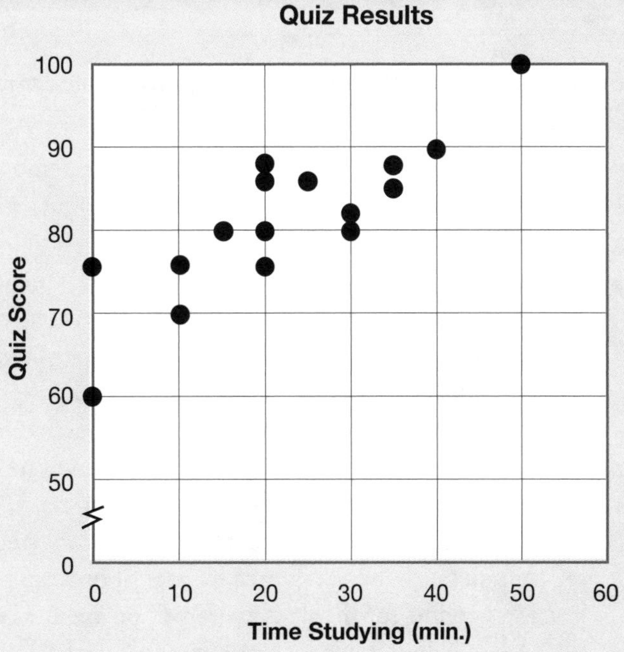

Fig. 4.24. Organizing data and using a scatter plot to explore a relationship between quiz score and time spent studying

Students notice that there appear to be sixteen dots in the scatter plot rather than twenty because repeated ordered pairs, such as (20, 80), are represented with a single point. However, it is important to keep a record that this point is a combination of three data points when using the display to interpret the data.

As students study different scatter plots, teachers should emphasize that the patterns of the dots can help students observe trends in data. For example, if the data cluster in an ascending pattern, a positive correlation exists. If the dots cluster in a descending pattern, a negative correlation exists. If the dots do not cluster but are scattered about the graph, there is no correlation. These correlations are summarized in figure 4.25.

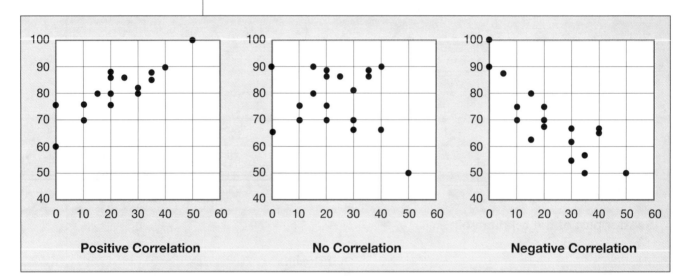

Fig. 4.25. Scatter plot dot patterns that show positive, negative, or no correlation in bivariate data

When there is a positive trend, for the most part, as values of one variable increase, values of the other variable also increase. When there is a negative trend, for the most part, as values of one variable increase, values of the other variable decrease. When there is no trend, the increase or decrease of the values for one variable does not affect the values of the other variable.

Students learn that they can draw a *trend line* to approximate the relationship. A trend line follows the general pattern of the dots, as shown in figure 4.26.

Teachers should point out that a trend line represents a set of bivariate data just as a measure of center or spread represents a set of univariate data. Although a measure of center or spread is a single number, a trend line is a set of points (that corresponds to a set of ordered pairs). Generally, if a trend line is a good fit for the data, there will be about as many data points above the line as below it. Note that this means that the point in the scatter plot that represents three data points counts three times and has a stronger influence on the trend than do the other points. The trend line that most closely models the set of bivariate data is called the *line of best fit*. Every other trend line

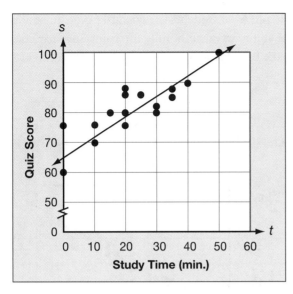

Fig. 4.26. Trend line for quiz-result data

for a set of data is an approximation for the line of best fit for that set of data. In later grades, students will use more advanced mathematics to find the line of best fit for a scatter plot.

During their study of bivariate data, students should have the opportunity to analyze scatter plots and trend lines. Teachers should structure experiences so that students learn that a trend line can be used to estimate or predict values that are not in the actual data set. For example, the point (45, 95) is a point on the trend line, so it is reasonable to estimate that if a student studies for forty-five minutes, his or her score will be about a 95, as shown in figure 4.27.

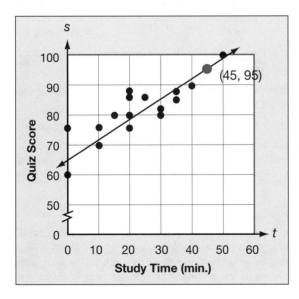

Fig. 4.27. Using a trend line to predict data

Teachers should have students study scatter plots in context so that they can develop the ability to meaningfully interpret, summarize, and analyze the data used to make the plot, as shown in the examples in figure 4.28.

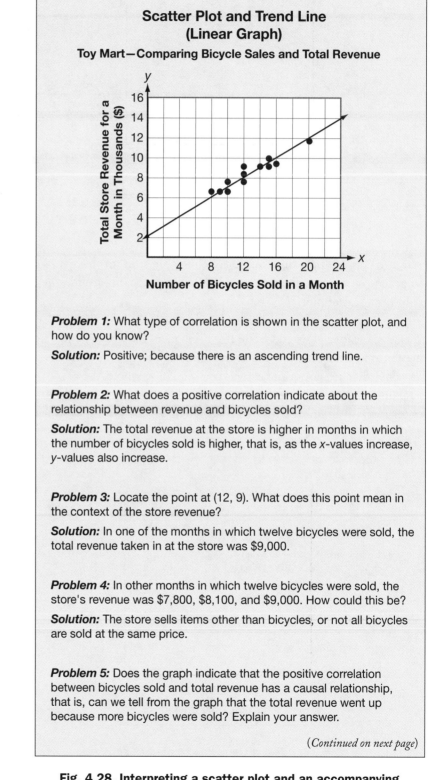

Problem 1: What type of correlation is shown in the scatter plot, and how do you know?

Solution: Positive; because there is an ascending trend line.

Problem 2: What does a positive correlation indicate about the relationship between revenue and bicycles sold?

Solution: The total revenue at the store is higher in months in which the number of bicycles sold is higher, that is, as the x-values increase, y-values also increase.

Problem 3: Locate the point at (12, 9). What does this point mean in the context of the store revenue?

Solution: In one of the months in which twelve bicycles were sold, the total revenue taken in at the store was $9,000.

Problem 4: In other months in which twelve bicycles were sold, the store's revenue was $7,800, $8,100, and $9,000. How could this be?

Solution: The store sells items other than bicycles, or not all bicycles are sold at the same price.

Problem 5: Does the graph indicate that the positive correlation between bicycles sold and total revenue has a causal relationship, that is, can we tell from the graph that the total revenue went up because more bicycles were sold? Explain your answer.

(Continued on next page)

Fig. 4.28. Interpreting a scatter plot and an accompanying trend line

> *Solution:* No; we can only tell that the total revenue went up when more bicycles were sold, not that it went up because more bicycles were sold. There might be other factors that would influence the total revenue, for example, the increase in revenue could have been caused by an increase in total purchases due to a holiday season or a store promotional sale designed to attract customers.
>
> *Problem 6:* Use the trend line to predict the total revenue if eighteen bicycles are sold one month. Explain your reasoning.
>
> *Solution:* About $11,000; the line passes through the point (18, 11).

Fig. 4.28. Interpreting a scatter plot and an accompanying trend line—*Continued*

Focusing on Analyzing and Summarizing Data Sets through Problem Solving

In a curriculum that is focused on analyzing and summarizing data, students will benefit from working with data in context. Thus, most of students' work will be constructed in problem-solving situations. When students are asked to create or analyze bar graphs, line graphs, line plots, stem-and-leaf plots, circle graphs, histograms, pictographs, box-and-whisker plots, or scatter plots, the given data or graph should be part of a problem to be solved or situation to be analyzed. The same applies when students are asked to find a measure of center or spread or to draw and use a trend line in a scatter plot—they should be given the task as part of a problem to be solved or situation to be analyzed, as exemplified in the previous sections.

Although students' initial experiences with the concepts in this Focal Point should include situations involving whole numbers and numbers that are easy to work with, as students' understanding of data displays and descriptive statistics deepens, data sets that include rational numbers, including decimals and fractions, should be introduced. Students' understanding of rational numbers can be reinforced through their work analyzing and summarizing data sets.

Focusing on Analyzing and Summarizing Data Sets through Connections

As students extend their study of data analysis and graphing, they should be given opportunities to make various connections to other mathematical concepts, for example, to linear functions. They should also be made aware of the connections of data analysis and graphing to the other subjects and to the world around them. For example, students should become aware of how data are used in science and social studies, as well as in newspapers, in magazines, and on the Internet. They should also learn of different ways in which graphs can be unintentionally or intentionally misleading.

Students apply their understanding of linear functions when they draw a trend line in a scatter plot of bivariate data, derive an equation for a trend line (also called a *line of fit*), or use the line or equation to make conjectures about the data. They should recognize that a scatter plot is a graph of a relation; if all data points fall on a line, then that is the line of best fit for the data and it is the graph of a linear function. Understanding linear functions will also help students use a trend line by allowing them to find an intercept or a slope. In a problem-solving situation, an intercept tells the value of one variable when the value of the other variable is zero, and the slope represents the rate of change of the dependent variable with respect to the independent variable. For example, in figure 4.29, the y-intercept is 2, indicating that, according to the trend line, the prediction for the total revenue is $2,000 in a month if no bicycles are sold. The slope is 0.5, indicating that, according to the trend line, the total revenue increases by about 0.5 thousand dollars ($500) for every bicycle sold.

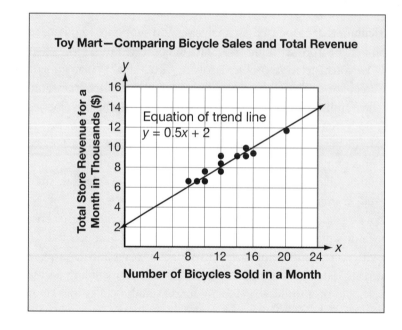

Fig. 4.29. Scatter plot and trend line

It is important that students understand that a trend line or line of best fit is only a *model* for a situation. Models are useful for analyzing, predicting, and inferring, but predictions and inferences based on models are not guaranteed to be accurate. For example, a student might infer that the slope in figure 4.29 indicates that the price of a bicycle is $500, but in reality the bicycle prices probably vary, with $500 being an average (mean) price. In some cases predictions and inferences may be misleading. The trend line in figure 4.29 matches the data very well and is very close to being the line of best fit for values between $x = 8$ and $x = 16$. However, inferences or predictions for values much greater than or much less than these values of x may not be as reliable. For example, according to the trend line, the total revenue in a month if no bicycles are sold would be $2,000. But if no bicycles are sold, it is possible that business overall that month would be very slow, and the total revenue might not be nearly $2,000.

As students examine graphs from various sources, they may begin to get a sense that graphs can be misleading. Sometimes graphs are unintentionally misleading; however, graphs may be designed to be purposefully misleading to sway opinion. One way to create a potentially misleading graph is to make the range on the vertical scale much greater than necessary, using a much greater number for the top of the scale than the greatest data value, thus minimizing the appearance of the distance between extreme data values. Another way is to insert a break in the vertical axis, thus exaggerating the representation of the distance between data values, as shown in figure 4.30.

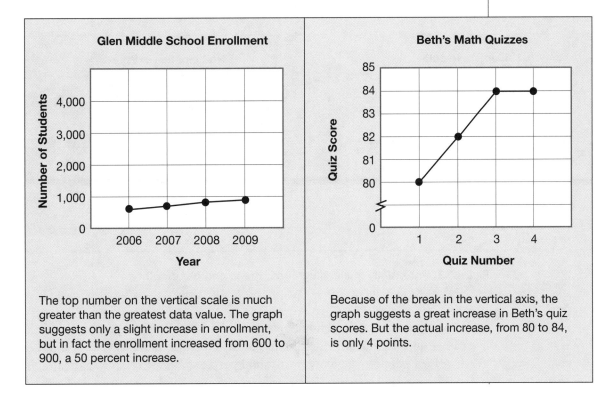

The top number on the vertical scale is much greater than the greatest data value. The graph suggests only a slight increase in enrollment, but in fact the enrollment increased from 600 to 900, a 50 percent increase.

Because of the break in the vertical axis, the graph suggests a great increase in Beth's quiz scores. But the actual increase, from 80 to 84, is only 4 points.

Fig. 4.30. Potentially misleading line graphs

Students need to develop the ability to judge whether a graph fairly represents the data and whether the graph has been created to purposefully mislead. For example, referring back to the enrollment graph in figure 4.30, students should think about possible reasons why the graph was made with such a large scale. They should ask themselves questions such as "Is there any reason why this graph would have been made to make it look like the change in enrollment was not significant?" If so, for example, if a school board wants to minimize the appearance of the increase in enrollment to justify not needing to spend money to build a new school, students need to consider these factors as they analyze and summarize the data. Thus, students need to become critical thinkers when analyzing graphs, using the mathematics that they have learned as well as their own understanding of the issues related to the context of the graph. The idea that data and statistics can be and are often used to persuade is one that students should focus on as they study the data and statistics in this Focal Point.

Three-dimensional or "tilted" graphs can also be potentially misleading. For example, a three-dimensional circle graph may not accurately show relative sizes of categories, as shown in figure 4.31. In this circle graph, Conrad received 39 votes and Ames received 32 votes, but the tilt of the graph makes it seem like Conrad got many more votes than the other candidates. In a three-dimensional bar graph, it can be difficult to determine the height of the bars. A first glance at the three-dimensional bar graph in figure 4.31 might suggest that the bar height for soccer is about 80, but in fact it is 90.

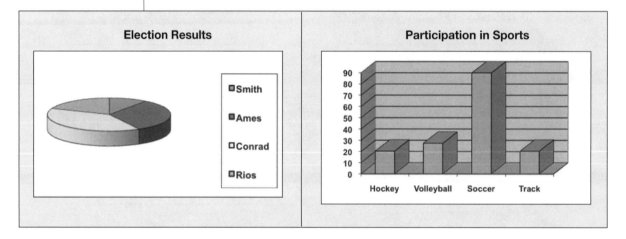

Fig. 4.31. Potentially misleading circle graph and bar graph

Students at grade 8 should recognize that their data and graphing skills can be applied in many other subject areas, especially in social studies and science. For example, students create and interpret graphs that show agricultural and industrial production, population trends, land and water areas, soil erosion, and fish and wildlife populations.

Students will also notice that data and statistics are prevalent in the world around them outside of their school subjects, for instance in print and electronic media. They should realize that people use data and statistics to make social, political, and economic decisions. Students will use the ability to analyze and summarize data that they develop in grade 8 to interpret graphs and numerical statistics and to make critical analyses about the accuracy of data displays throughout their lives. A broad and deep understanding of data and statistics will enable students to interpret data themselves instead of having to rely on the interpretations of others.

Connections in later grades

In later grades students will continue to develop their ability to analyze and summarize data sets using data displays and descriptive statistics. For example, in later grades students formulate questions that can be addressed with data they collect. Then they organize and display relevant data to answer these questions. Students learn the importance of sampling to gather information about a population; that is, they learn how to choose part of the population, called a *sample*, and gather data from that sample. They study various sampling methods, such as random, stratified random, systematic, convenience, and self-selected sampling. They also learn that samples must be representative of the group for their results to be valid and how to extrapolate their results from the sample to the entire group.

In later grades, students learn additional statistical methods to select from and use to analyze data. They learn that one important way data values can vary consistently from the mean is in a normal distribution. The graphs of normal distributions are symmetrical bell-shaped curves. Fifty percent of the distribution lies to the left of the mean and 50 percent lies to the right of the mean, as shown in figure 4.32. They also learn about a measure of variation (measure of spread) called the *standard deviation*, which is a measure of how much the values in a data set vary, or deviate, from the mean.

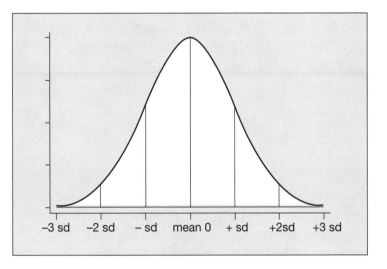

Fig. 4.32. Normal distribution curve

In later grades, students also learn that a numerical data value has an associated percentile, which indicates the percent of the data that is less than or equal to that data value. For example, if a student's grade point average is at the 65th percentile compared with all the students in the school, then that student's grade-point average is greater than or equal to 65 percent of the grade-point averages of all the other students in the school. Students will also study outliers—data values that are much greater or much less than the rest of the data set. They might learn that an outlier is often defined as a data value that is outside the middle half of the data by more than 1.5 times the interquartile range, that is, less than $Q_1 - 1.5(IQR)$ or greater than $Q_1 + 1.5(IQR)$.

Students will continue to develop and evaluate inferences and predictions that are based on data. For example, they will learn that the margin of error is an estimate of the amount of error associated with a sample proportion—if a poll shows 60 percent of voters in favor of a candidate with a margin of error of ±4%, then students can infer that it is likely that 56 percent to 64 percent of the overall population of voters is in favor of that candidate. To evaluate this inference, students need to know details of the methods for obtaining the data, for example, how the sample was selected.

Students will study basic concepts of probability. They will learn that experimental probability is based on observations or results of an experiment. Each observation or performance of the experiment is called a *trial*, and the experimental probability of an event is defined as

$$\frac{\text{number of times the envent occurs}}{\text{number of trials}}.$$

For example, if you draw a marble from a bag at random fifty times, replacing the marble after each draw, and get a red marble ten times, then the experimental probability of drawing a red marble from that bag is 10/50, or 1/5. Students will learn that theoretical probability is based on a sample space; if a sample space has n equally likely outcomes, then the theoretical probability of an event E is defined as

$$\frac{\text{number of outcomes in } E}{n}.$$

Suppose a bag contains forty marbles—ten red, ten black, and twenty white. Then the theoretical probability of drawing a red marble from that bag is 10/40, or 1/4. Students will also learn about some other basic concepts of probability, including dependent and independent events, mutually exclusive events, geometric probability, and probability distributions.

Developing Depth of Understanding

How can you, in your classroom, help students understand and be able to describe strengths and weaknesses of the different data displays and statistical measures? What activities can you do in your classroom to help students decide which display or measure they can use to accurately display their data?

References

Donovan, M. Suzanne, and John D. Bransford, eds. *How Students Learn: Mathematics in the Classroom.* Washington, D.C.: National Research Council, 2005.

Franklin, Christine, Gary Kader, Denise Mewborn, Jerry Moreno, Roxy Peck, Mike Perry, and Richard Scheaffer. *Guidelines for Assessment and Instruction in Statistics Education (GAISE) Report: A Pre-K-12 Curriculum Framework.* Alexandria, Va.: American Statistical Association, 2007.

Fuson, Karen C., and Aki Murata. "Integrating the NRC Principles and the NCTM Process Standards: Cognitively Guided Teaching to Individualize Instruction within Whole-Class Activities and Move All Students within Their Learning Path." *National Council of Supervisors of Mathematics Journal* 10 (Spring 2007): 72–91.

Kilpatrick, Jeremy, Jane Swafford, and Bradford Findell. *Adding It Up: Helping Children Learn Mathematics.* Washington, D.C.: National Research Council, 2001.

Lampert, Magdalene. "Choosing and Using Mathematical Tools in Classroom Discourse." In *Advances in Research on Teaching,* vol. 1, edited by Jere Brophy, pp. 223–64. Greenwich, Conn.: JAI Press, 1989.

Mack, Nancy K. "Learning Fractions with Understanding: Building on Informal Knowledge." *Journal for Research in Mathematics Education* 21 (January 1990): 16–32.

Mirra, Amy. *Focus in Grades 6–8: Teaching with Curriculum Focal Points.* Reston, Va.: National Council of Teachers of Mathematics, 2009.

National Council of Teachers of Mathematics (NCTM). *Curriculum and Evaluation Standards for School Mathematics.* Reston, Va.: NCTM, 1989.

_____. *Principles and Standards for School Mathematics.* Reston, Va.: NCTM, 2000.

_____. *Curriculum Focal Points for Prekindergarten through Grade 8 Mathematics: A Quest for Coherence.* Reston, Va.: NCTM, 2006.

_____. *Focus in Grade 3.* Reston, Va.: NCTM, 2009.

_____. *Focus in Grade 4.* Reston, Va.: NCTM, 2009.

_____. *Focus in High School Mathematics: Reasoning and Sense Making.* Reston, Va.: NCTM, 2009.

_____. *Focus in Grade 6.* Reston, Va.: NCTM, 2010.

_____. *Focus in Grade 7.* Reston, Va.: NCTM, 2010.

Rachlin, Sid, Kathleen Cramer, Connie Finseth, Linda Cooper Foreman, Dorothy Geary, Seth Leavitt, and Margaret Schwan Smith. *Navigating through Number and Operations in Grades 6–8.* Reston, Va.: National Council of Teachers of Mathematics, 2006.

Webb, David C., Nina Boswinkel, and Truus Dekker. "Beneath the Tip of the Iceberg: Using Representations to Support Student Understanding." *Mathematics Teaching in the Middle School* 14 (September 2008): 110–13.